CRAVING LOVE

KAT T. MASEN

Kat T. Masen

Craving Love

An Age Gap Romance
The Secret Love Series Book 1

Copyright 2022 Kat T. Masen
All Rights Reserved

Disclaimer: The material in this book contains graphic language and sexual content and is intended for mature audiences, ages 18 and older.

ISBN: 979-8364392572

Editing by More Than Words Copyediting and Proofreading
Cover design by The Book Cover Boutique
Cover Image Copyright 2022
First Edition 2022
All Rights Reserved

NOTE TO READER

Craving Love is the first book in The Secret Love Series.
This book is best read after The Dark Love or Forbidden
Love Series.
Some of the characters in this book are from previous works.
To best understand the dynamics of the Edwards family, it's
highly recommended to begin with *Chasing Love*.

However, Alexa's story is untold.
You can still enjoy this as a standalone, bearing in mind her
family has quite the history.
Love triangles, secret pregnancies, forbidden romances...
just the usual plots I'm known to write.

ONE

"I'm guessing Daddy didn't see you leaving the house like this?"

A sigh escapes me. Another party, another night of faking it with people I don't particularly like. All because I'm supposed to be a team player—stay social so people will like me.

Cole grabs my hand as we enter the crowded house for Mikayla's eighteenth birthday party. Considering it's a school night, everyone from senior year is here. Apparently, the reason behind the Thursday night party is because Mikayla's parents are taking her to Europe tomorrow. If only we all had such relaxed parents.

"He didn't see me," I say over the loud music. "I left before he came home."

Cole leans in, brushing his lips against my ear. *"I want to fuck you in this dress."*

I force a fake smile as we walk into the large living room, pretending the compliment makes me happy. Cole looks handsome tonight, dressed in a white tee with a gold chain around his neck. His white Nike sneakers are brand new, standing out against his dark denim jeans. He's always been a great dresser, and his sneaker collection is next level. Cole will drop a lot of money on shoes, especially if they're rare. Luckily, his parents support his expensive habit and don't mind spoiling him.

He runs his hand through his black hair, nodding to greet people but then stops and says hello to his friends. Most of them are from the football team, jocks just like him.

Hanging out with the boys can get tedious since all they talk about is chicks they want to screw. Half the girls wouldn't touch these guys for the life of them. The newest challenge they set upon themselves is trying to take the virginity of some new girl. All I know is that she's quiet and keeps to herself. She does come across as nerdy with her thick black glasses and weird obsession with wearing plaid, but nevertheless, his friends have no chance.

Five minutes into hanging around the guys, and I'm already bored. This always happens, so it doesn't surprise me anymore. I excuse myself to walk around, saying hello to a few friends before making my way outside to the pool. I'm surprised by how many people are in the water and not so surprised when I see a guy throwing up on the side.

It's a warm enough night to swim. I'm not exactly dressed for it, already pushing my limits with the dress I wear. It dawned on me a pair of jeans would have been much more comfortable, but I wanted to prove a point to myself.

Life can go back to normal.

I can move on.

It's been months.

Near the outdoor grill is a table with drinks. It's obvious the punch is spiked, which is why it's popular, and people keep helping themselves. I contemplate having a drink, but my mood doesn't call for it. The last time I drank didn't end well. I vomited in Cole's car, and he had to clean me up. He tried his best but then called Ava to come help since my dress was ruined, and I wasn't able to stay awake. She made up some lie to my parents about staying over at her place, ultimately saving me.

A set of arms wraps around my waist as the familiar cologne lingers. My chest rises, then falls, remembering all the good times we have had over the last year since we started dating.

It wasn't always bad, or maybe I mean to say—I wasn't always like this.

"Let's go upstairs," Cole suggests with a flirtatious tone. "I want you alone."

There is only so much I can say to distract him, but I try anyway.

"There are a lot of people. I'm sure the rooms are occupied."

He leans in to whisper, "There's a secret room no one knows about."

My eyes wander to the pink-colored punch floating in the large bowl. With a deep breath, I pour myself a cup and drink it in one go. A rasp escapes me, the alcohol content stronger than anticipated. It's so bad, I'm pretty sure there's more than one type mixed in here.

Cole laughs, then does the same. Unlike me, he holds his drinks much better.

Without another word, Cole grabs my hand and leads me to a flight of stairs near the kitchen. The house is big, though not as big as mine, and I have no clue where he is taking me.

Down the long hallway, there are several doors, but

Cole opens the one all the way at the end. The room itself appears to be a guest room. Its furnishings are minimal, with a king-size bed being the room's focus.

It feels like déjà vu.

The night when my life changed, our lives changed. Though, he had no idea.

Cole closes the door behind me, leading us to the bed. He doesn't waste any time, pressing his lips against mine forcefully. His hands wander beneath my dress, causing me to tense. *Just get it over and done with, I beg myself.*

"What's wrong?" Cole pulls back. "Why don't you want me to fuck you?"

Another moment where I can tell him the truth just like all the other moments which presented themselves. But what's the point? It's over, and everything should go back to normal.

He won't care, or at least he'll pretend to care, but none of it matters since it won't change the outcome.

"I've got a lot on my mind," I half tell the truth.

"Someone else is on your mind?"

"Cole, there's no one else. It's only been you."

Unlike many girls in senior year, I've only been with one guy. I've kissed several boys, but none were worthy of going to the next base until Cole came along.

"Yeah, well, you're making me feel like shit," he complains.

I pull back, resting on my elbows. "Just because I don't feel like fucking you?"

Cole jumps off the bed, pacing with his hands running through his hair. His blue eyes watch me, almost as if I'm doing something wrong by not giving in to him tonight. *He doesn't understand. He'll never understand.*

Suddenly, a piercing scream startles us both. It came from outside, so I run to the window to see what is happening. My eyes widen in shock as a body is dragged from the pool, unconscious.

Without a second thought, I bolt out of the room, leaving Cole behind as adrenaline runs through my veins. The fresh air hits my face when I make it outside, but I rush to the scene.

"Someone call 9-1-1!"

People gather around the boy lying unconscious by the side of the pool. They uselessly stare in bewilderment, but no one does a damn thing. I push people aside, then fall to my knees to examine him.

I'd watched a YouTube video on how to perform CPR. It was one of those nights I fell down a rabbit hole leading me to medical videos. I was fascinated with it all, unsure why but hoping it would stick.

Remembering each step, I attempt to perform CPR. Thankfully, he has a pulse, but how long depends on what I do next.

I hear the voice in my head repeating the steps. As people watch on, I begin with the chest compressions using my body weight and keeping my arms straight, then press straight down. Next, I release the pressure before giving mouth-to-mouth.

"Alexa, what the fuck are you doing?" Cole questions angrily.

"Paramedics will be here any minute."

Another minute and we might lose him.

Don't let this happen.

I place one hand on his forehead and the other under his chin to tilt the head back so his airways open. Pinching the soft part of his nose so it closes, I open his mouth with my thumb and fingers.

As I take a breath, Cole continues to yell at me, but I ignore him, placing my lips over the guy's mouth and blowing steadily. When I pull back, a rough cough escapes his lips before he shuffles to his side and starts expelling water.

"Alexa," Mikayla cries, pressing on my shoulders. "You saved him!"

Still on my knees, I sit back and watch as the guy opens his eyes, disoriented. The paramedics arrive, running through the crowd with their equipment. The noise fades out, the scene becoming a sudden blur.

"You saved his life," the paramedic praises as they continue to examine him. "Ever considered a career in medicine?"

Cole deliberately raises his brows while cocking his head. "Dr. Edwards, just like Daddy."

His callous comment strikes a nerve with me. The memories come flashing back, the times I'd begged my older sisters to play hospital with me after I'd stolen Dad's stethoscope from his office drawer.

But I'd rather die than fall hostage to my father's hopes and dreams for me.

"I'm glad he's alive," I mutter under my breath. "I want to go home."

Cole crosses his arms in defiance. "Well, I want to stay."

I turn my back on him and ignore everyone as I make my way outside. Reaching for my purse, I open the Uber app, but it shows no one available. Just fucking great.

Scrolling through my phone, I realize all my sisters flew out tonight to Cancun. There's no chance in hell I'm calling my parents since I'm already in trouble, given all Mom's messages. I dial my cousin Luna's number, and thankfully she picks up.

Twenty minutes later, we're on the way home.

"Does Uncle Lex know you're out this late on a school night?" Luna asks, pulling into my street.

"I'll deal with it tomorrow."

"Aren't you afraid of being grounded?"

I shrug. "Not really."

As we pull into the driveway, Luna leaves the car running. "You sure you don't want to talk about it?"

"I'm fine. Thanks again."

With my purse in hand, I exit the car and take a deep breath. If all goes well, I can run up to my room so I'm not caught in this short yellow dress I borrowed from Ava.

The second I step inside, I turn the light on to see my father. His presence in the darkness catches me by surprise, and his eyes turn angry upon noticing my dress.

"Oh," I mouth, avoiding eye contact.

"Oh?" he repeats in a cold tone. "Is that the only response I'll get from you, considering it's two hours past your curfew, and it's a school night?"

Growing up as the youngest daughter of a well-known billionaire is not glamorous like everyone thinks it is.

My father, Lex Edwards, controls everything our family does. My sisters may have moved out, but I'm the last one under his wrath.

God forbid I do anything to disobey him. He demands respect, but I'm so over his controlling ways. I continue to ignore him, flicking my long hair over my shoulder in complete disregard for his authority.

"Anything you'd like to say, Alexandra?"

A puff of air leaves my lips as I roll my eyes in annoyance.

"Let me guess. You're calling me Alexandra, so I'm in big trouble? Assuming I'm grounded, you'll take all my privileges from me because you are the controlling Lex Edwards."

His eyes widen as his nostrils flare. Lowering his gaze for a moment, he's obviously trying to control himself because Mom told him to.

"You're damn right you're grounded," he shouts, slamming his fist on the counter. "How dare you worry your mother and me over your careless actions. You live in this house. You abide by our rules."

Of course, he has no sympathy. He has no idea what happened tonight, and even if I told him the truth, he'd find a way to turn it into all about his rules.

"I'm over your rules!" I yell back, eyes blazing with fire. "I didn't ask to be Lex Edwards' daughter. This life was thrust upon me."

"This life?" He tilts his head in confusion. "A life of having a roof over your head, food on the table, and private schooling? I'm sorry. Please explain how awful it is for you to have what many children have to fight for."

If only he knew the truth.

I drop my eyes to the floor. "You have no idea."

"No idea how spoiled you are? You have everything you want. Please, enlighten me. How terrible it is to grow up as our daughter?"

Slowly, I lift my gaze to meet his matching emerald eyes. He waits for me to respond, but what is there to say?

"I hate you."

And as quick as the words leave my mouth, I exit the kitchen and run up to my bedroom. Shutting the door behind me, I lean back against it as tears fall down my cheeks.

It's all his fault.

I aborted Cole's baby because of him.

And now, I must live with this decision for the rest of my life.

All because I carry the Edwards' name.

TWO

It's been weeks since the fight with my father.

He's sitting at the head of the patio table with Mom beside him. They both wait for me to begin since I'd called this meeting after my sisters and their families left.

It's now or never. I'm carrying the gasoline to throw on the already burning fire between us. I spread my hands out on the table, unable to look at either of them. A small breath escapes me while I muster the courage to follow through with what I want for my life.

Breathe... one... two... three.

"I've decided not to go to college," I state firmly.

As expected, silence falls between us. I keep my eyes fixed on the centerpiece and avoid looking at my father. If it was possible to smell smoke coming out of someone's ears, I'm smelling the burning smoke right now and choking on it.

"Alexa," Mom stammers, "I... I don't understand where this is coming from?"

"This is coming from someone who doesn't want to go

to college," I respond matter-of-factly. "Just because my sisters went doesn't mean I have to."

Mom stares in confusion. "So, what exactly will you be doing?"

"I'll be traveling around Europe."

"Then, when you're done, say, in a year? You're going to enroll?" Mom pushes.

In slow motion, I raise my eyes to meet my father's. The skin around his eyes tightens as his jaw sets. "No."

More silence, of course. No one defies Lex Edwards, yet here I am.

"You have one year to travel," he states in an arctic tone, his voice strangled while trying to control his temper. "Then, you will return and enroll in college."

I stand up in a rush, crossing my arms with a defiant stare. "You don't get a say in my life anymore. I'm almost eighteen."

"As long as you live under this roof," he threatens.

"Well, guess what, Lex..." I drag his name in a condescending tone. "As soon as I graduate, I will no longer be living under this roof. You can control what you want, but you will never control me."

The anger of this conversation forces me to leave and run inside the house away from him and his empty threats. My steps move fast up the stairs, almost tripping halfway up the staircase.

The door to my bedroom slams shut with a loud thud causing the picture frames on the wall to shake from the vibration.

My heart races a million miles, unable to slow down to a normal pace. This decision has been weighing heavily on my mind of late. The more we argued and he laid down new rules, the more I wanted to defy him.

Slowly, I rest my head against the door while my eyes close to calm myself down. The temperature inside the room is warmer than usual despite my window being open. There's a soft nightly breeze, but it's not enough to cool my heated skin.

No one goes against the great *Lex Edwards*.

I'd seen people attempt, but they never succeeded. There had been times I'd overheard my father talking to Mom about some business conflict. It wasn't unusual for him to encounter people who made it their mission to destroy the successful billionaire. But, in the end, my father always played his cards right and won.

That was business, and I'm family.

My eyes open wide, staring directly into my bedroom, a haven from all the chaos in my life. The king-size bed is perfectly made with my favorite ivory bedspread. When it came to aesthetics, my bedroom styling changed as quickly as my mood. Right now, I'm going through my neutral phase, which beats the emo-dark phase I went through in junior high.

The desk sitting opposite my bed is paired with a velvet cream armchair. My MacBook sits on the desk along with some books I need to finish reading. Reading wasn't my thing until a few months ago when I stumbled on a book that had the worst reviews. Naturally, I wanted to know what all the negative hype was about. It turned out I loved it, then binge-read the whole series. Reading became a sort of escapism, and these books were nothing like the boring novels we were forced to read in school.

The spice was next level, and things I never knew existed opened my eyes to a whole other world. It's not like I hadn't had sex. I just hadn't had sex like the characters in a *book*.

Above the desk is a corkboard with photos pinned on it. There are many of Cole, some of us, and a few with friends.

My feet move toward the desk to observe the photos closer. They are all memories from a time when life was less complicated—at the beginning of my senior year, when I had all these hopes and dreams, thinking it would be the best year of my life.

Friends came and went, which is totally the norm in high school—but I never expected my family to be the reason why people wanted my friendship. If my father was a billionaire, then apparently, so was I. Not only were they hung up on wealth, but they were also hung up on my father to the point I was often bullied. I'd walk the halls and be cornered by a bunch of mean girls who would go into detail about their sexual fantasies involving my father.

Their obsession with him got more and more gross as time went on.

Another reason why my resentment grew deeper and why I couldn't talk to my parents. What would they say? *Grow a backbone, Alexa. Life ain't easy.*

Then, there is Cole—my boyfriend.

Our relationship has been strained since the night of the party. The arguments between us escalated over the dumbest reasons. He was embarrassed I'd saved the life of another guy. It was the stupidest thing I'd ever heard. Cole should have said he was jealous because I performed CPR, including mouth-to-mouth. I mean, it's not like I kissed him. The more I think about it, the more annoyed I become. His immaturity is shining through, which is why I made certain decisions.

As for college, Cole has no idea I've been thinking about traveling. He has his whole college life planned out. Frat house, keg parties, and our break-up is inevitable since our views on the next four years are the complete opposite.

He wants to party and... *I don't know what I want.*

A gentle knock breaks me from my thoughts. I know it's Mom, and even though I'm not in the mood, she's not the one I'm angry at.

"Come in," I mutter.

The door opens as Mom steps in, softly closing the door behind her. My mother is a very beautiful woman with classic features, which makes her appear ageless. Yet as our eyes meet for a brief moment, I notice the tired expression on her face but quickly glance away to pretend I don't care.

"I don't understand where this is all coming from, Alexa," she begins in an exasperated voice. "This attitude and disrespect for our family."

"I'm not disrespecting our family," I answer defensively while crossing my arms in defiance. "I've been nothing but nice to you."

Her lips purse into a white sash. "Your father doesn't deserve this."

"Right..." I drag with a twisted mouth. "Because the great Lex Edwards always gets what he wants."

It's Mom's turn to cross her arms, shaking her head with obvious disappointment. I should have known she would defend her husband over me. *What's fucking new in this family.*

Mom points her finger with a stern gaze. "Don't you dare spin whatever the hell is going on with you and blame our family. You've been given a life many girls would die for, and here you are treating us like we've done you wrong."

I'm taken aback by Mom's raised tone, given the only

time she's fought with me is over petty things like me taking something from her closet without asking.

"Are we done?"

"Alexa," Mom softens but drops her gaze to the ground. "You need to talk about whatever it is that is bothering you... whatever it is that has happened to you."

Mom would never understand. So what if I told her I'd fallen pregnant to Cole but chose to abort the baby because everyone would blame me for ruining their life? What difference would it make now?

It's over.

"I want to be alone, please."

I turn my back to face the window and stare into the dark night. Behind me, the door closes, and Mom is gone without another word.

The weight of tonight leaves me exhausted. I take a long shower hoping to relax enough to fall asleep. Like all nights, my eyes grow weary, and I fall asleep within minutes.

But then, the nightmare begins.

I'm lying on the hard bed, alone, staring up at the fluorescent light. Thoughts run rampant, confusing me and leaving me terrified. The nurses enter the room and start prepping, talking amongst themselves, and one even laughs.

I keep thinking about my choice. What if I say no? What if I choose to have the baby? But the fear, it consumes me to the point of silence.

One nurse stops and explains what is going to happen next.

The baby is going to die.

This is my fault.

My body jerks forward as my chest rises and falls, barely able to catch a breath. It's the middle of the night, and my room is pitch black. I shut my eyes tight, wishing this would go away, then fall back onto the bed.

I toss and turn, finally falling asleep at the crack of dawn before it's time to wake up for school.

The school day drags on, as does my exhaustion. I almost fall asleep in bio, but thankfully the girl sitting next to me nudges me before Miss Dawson walks over.

Cole is busy with his friends, which I kind of welcome since he'd want me to come to his place after school. His parents are always working, making it easy for us to have sex without worrying about getting caught. But lately, I've tried to come up with every excuse to avoid it.

When I get back home, the house is empty. I grab a bag of Reese's from the pantry, then head to my room to enjoy the peace and quiet.

As I open the door, I stop dead in my tracks.

My two older sisters, Millie and Ava, sit in my room without a care. My other sister, Addy, lives in San Francisco, so it comes as no surprise she hasn't joined forces with Millie and Ava.

"You have a hell of a lot of explaining to do," Ava utters.

Ava is my father's favorite daughter. Everyone in the family knows that. Of course, she will defend him and make it out like I'm the villain. There's no point talking to my sisters like they'd even understand. Both are married, have kids, and don't live under these stupid rules my parents insist on having.

Ignoring them, I walk toward my desk, swing my bag over the chair, and place my books on my desk.

"This is my room, and you weren't invited in," I respond in frustration.

Ava and Millie glance at each other. I'm waiting for Ava to go psycho since she has no filter, but Millie can hold an argument without backing down since she's an attorney like Mom.

"You hurt Dad. Just so you know," Ava blurts out.

"The man is invincible," I mutter, kicking my shoes off and walking to my closet to change out of my uniform. I settle on a pair of sweats, even though it's hot out, and my favorite tee. When I step back into my room, my sisters are less than pleased by my disregard for them defending my father.

"Dad aside..." Millie begins to pause briefly, then continues, "... why don't you want to go to college? You do realize without a college degree your career choice is limited."

I shrug, then throw myself onto my bed with my phone. "I want to travel."

"On whose money?" Ava shouts, unable to hold back her anger. "Mom and Dad's money?"

Over the many birthdays and special occasions, I'd put aside some cash for a just-in-case moment. My grandparents would spoil me rotten, gifting me envelopes on the sly despite my parents' wealth. I've saved a few thousand dollars to buy myself a plane ticket to Europe and a few weeks' stay at a low-budget hostel until I find a job. The hostel part isn't exactly appealing, but surely it can't be that bad.

"I have my own money, thank you very much."

"And, so what? You last like a month until you call Dad begging for help," Ava accuses.

I shuffle so my elbows rest on the bed, shifting my attention to my sisters. Millie is a lot like Mom in looks, the same brown shade of hair and facial features. Her eyes are identical to Dad's, just like all of us. However, Ava looks just like Dad, which is probably why she's the favorite.

"I think you're confusing me for you, Ava," I note with dark amusement.

Ava opens her mouth, but Millie grabs her arm to stop her.

"What about Cole?" Millie questions. "Are you going to break up with him?"

"I'm not like you, Millie. I don't hold onto high school boyfriends for the sake of it."

The moment Millie's eyes widened and her mouth falls open, I know I've struck a nerve. It's the truth, though. She stayed with her high school boyfriend and tried to do the whole long-distance thing until she cheated on him. Millie will argue she didn't cheat. They were already broken up. Whatever, like I care what she did in her love life.

"Now you're just being a bitch," Ava bellows.

"I'm tired." I yawn, ignoring them. "You've said what you came to say. Now leave."

I just want to be alone, away from my family and some other place where the nightmares don't follow me.

"You can run..." Millie says in a low voice, "... but one day, you're going to realize the people you pushed away are the ones you need the most."

And just like that, my sisters leave my room.

Millie is wrong. I don't need anyone. Soon, I'll be far away and starting a new life on my own. I'll make it work for as long as I can, even if it means I have to work hard to earn my own money to survive.

I don't need a man, nor do I need my father's help.

And the best part of my plan... no one will know I'm Lex Edwards' daughter.

I'll make damn sure of it.

THREE

"So, what? You're just going to take off like we're nothing?"

Cole's raised voice echoes around us as we sit on the sand, watching the waves. Something is calming about the ocean. One minute, a wave crashes against the shoreline, making its presence known, and the next, there's an eerie silence.

Rinse, cycle, repeat.

Just like this conversation.

I'm trying to understand why this conversation is a surprise to Cole. We haven't been the same since the party almost two months ago. He's busied himself with friends and God knows what. The boys were known to fuck whoever they could get their hands on. Cole had a history before he and I hooked up. He dated and slept with several girls.

Though he was my *first*.

It wasn't uncommon for rumors to travel of him cheating on me. For the most part, I blocked out all the noise, but deep down, it hurt. Just because I don't see a future with us doesn't mean his being with other girls is any easier to swallow.

I've been trying to study for finals despite not wanting to attend college. I mean, maybe one day I might change my mind, but as of right now, it's not for me.

"I'm not taking off like we're nothing," I tell him, unable to hide the disappointment in my voice. No matter what I do, Cole will never escape me. How can he when he got me pregnant at the age of seventeen? His memory will always be *something*. "We're so young."

"And your dad is okay with this?" he questions in disbelief.

Things with Dad could have been a lot worse. I suspected Mom has a lot to do with the fact that he's still even talking to me. Occasionally, we cross paths, and he brings up places to visit in Europe. I appear interested though his acceptance of my traveling is making me question my whole decision. By then, I usually mumble something and walk away disinterested because I don't like questioning my life choices.

"He's fine," I half-lie. "Well, he's fine now."

Suddenly, Cole stands up and distances himself. As he crosses his arms, his stare is fixated on the ocean. Then, he turns around with a clenched jaw, nostrils flaring like a bull ready to attack.

"Is there someone else?"

I shake my head while pursing my lips. "Why does it always have to be about someone else?"

"Because I haven't fucked you in forever!"

A sinking feeling forms in the pit of my stomach. Maybe that's all I'm good for, a quick fuck in the bedroom or my name attached to the Edwards' wealth.

Just when will someone see me for me?

"Silence speaks many words you can't seem to answer," he accuses with malice.

His wide eyes fixate on me. They're cold and uninviting, lacking the warmth and comfort I would have expected from someone who told me they loved me. I remember it like it was yesterday, the weighted words said right before I gave myself up.

Cole promised me the world, and I believed him.

Suddenly, he turns his back and begins walking away with not a single word left to say.

The breath I'd been holding in finally released. No matter what I do, I'm making everyone miserable, including myself. In just a few months, no one will have to worry about me because out of sight, out of mind.

I make my way home but stop at the drugstore for some products I ran out of. Somewhere in the deodorant aisle, my phone pings with a text message. I'm expecting it's Cole but also not surprised when I see it's my sisters in our group chat.

AVA

What happened with Cole?

How on Earth did she know I was meeting up with him? I swear my sister is some secret spy and knows everything before I can even get a word out.

ME

How did you know I was meeting him?

AVA

He texted me.

ME

And?

AVA

He thinks you're seeing someone else and
wanted me to tell him the truth. So,
are you?

ME

I'm not Millie...

MILLIE

Why does it always come back to me? You
know Mom and Dad aren't so innocent.
They had an affair... A BIG ONE, OKAY.

ADDY

Sometimes, in relationships, the force of
two people far outweighs the rationality of
crossing boundaries.

AVA

Here comes Miss Psych with her
relationship analysis.

ADDY

Alexa needs wisdom... not advice from
someone who had a one-night stand with
her sister's ex.

Our conversations always jumped back and forth at the expense of one of us. Like always, nasty words are said, and all is forgotten tomorrow. Even after Ava and Millie ambushed me last week, they carried on the next day like nothing had happened.

The only time we fought long enough to go without speaking was when Ava announced she was pregnant. I love her husband Austin like an older brother, but he was Millie's boyfriend turned fiancé first. Talk about shitting where you eat or whatever the stupid saying is.

> **ME**
>
> I'm not seeing anyone else. It's not going to work out. He's going to Ohio State, and I'm going to be away in Europe. What's the point of trying long distance when neither of us are willing to sacrifice our future?

ADDY

You shouldn't have to sacrifice what you want for a man. Period.

AVA

Speaking of periods… Millie's is late.

ADDY

Oh…

> **ME**
>
> Again???

MILLIE

AVA! Why do I tell you anything???

AVA

Maybe the parentals need to sit you down and give you the safe-sex talk LOL.

A heavy weight on my chest distracts me from the text messages. You can have all the safe-sex talks, but one misjudgment is all it takes.

One misjudgment is all it took for *me*.

We were drunk, at a party, inside a bedroom that belonged to someone's little brother. A series of events led me to make one bad decision after another. I should have known better, especially since Mom and my sisters were open when it came to discussing sex.

I place my phone back in my purse, needing a break from my sisters, and then head to the checkout to purchase my items. Before heading home, I stop to grab something to eat, realizing I'd skipped lunch at school to avoid the girls in the cafeteria. School has been such a toxic environment lately, so I can't wait to graduate and get out of there.

When I pull into the driveway, Dad's car is parked outside. It's early for him to be home, but what catches my attention is Cole's car beside it. *What the hell?* I quickly grab my things and slam the door shut before rushing to the back door and entering the kitchen.

Cole is standing next to the counter, shifting his gaze onto me as Dad sits across from him. I'm quick to notice Cole's glassy eyes, which is what happens when he drinks. How is that even possible since I saw him only an hour ago? Not to mention he drove here. Great, now he's going to get me into trouble.

"What are you doing here?" I ask, crossing my arms in annoyance.

"Talking to your dad about your decision not to go to college."

I tilt my head to the side. "Excuse me? You have no right coming into my home to discuss a decision that is mine."

"Just admit there's someone else," he says in a bitter tone.

On the countertop, his hand is clenched into a fist as jealousy consumes him. I'm so over his insecurity and immaturity. Why does it always have to involve another fucking guy? I can't believe this is happening in front of Dad, who sits there not saying a damn word.

"Leave," I mutter.

"Do you see what I mean, Mr. Edwards?" Cole snarls then shakes his head. "I guess this is it, huh?"

"Cole," Dad warns but pauses to control his own anger. He keeps his expression stern before continuing, "You need to calm down now."

This time, I bow my head. Even when your gut tells you the truth, the reality is sometimes far worse. It wasn't ever meant to last. We are two different people. It's another reason I chose not to go ahead with the pregnancy. Cole wasn't ready to be a dad, and if I had forced it upon him, he would have resented the baby and me. That's no way for a child to grow up.

"It was over a long time ago," I say in a whisper. "Don't make it harder than it has to be."

I'm half-expecting Cole to lash out, his temper worsening of late, but Dad being present is my saving grace. Without another word, he walks toward the door and slams the door behind him. The silence is short-lived as the sound of his engine roaring echoes in the kitchen. Then, on cue, the car accelerates out of the driveway, which I can only assume is not at a safe speed.

My palms lay flat on the countertop while I try to suppress the guilt trying to consume me. The more the guilt fights its way through, the more I feel this is all my fault.

"You made the right decision ending things," Dad speaks up rather calmly. "If traveling and exploring the world is what your heart is set on, then it's best you do it without the pressure of trying to hold onto a relationship."

I raise my eyes to meet his. Did he just accept me going away without his usual condescending tone? I'm taken aback, unsure what to say or do. After my outburst and telling him I hated him, I knew things between us were rocky. Even though he'd offer suggestions of where to go and what to see, I just thought that was small talk.

If this is the olive branch, then maybe it wouldn't hurt for me to extend mine, just like he has done because right now, I'm tired of fighting all these battles.

"I don't hate you," I admit in a low voice. "The night of

the party, someone drowned. Everyone panicked, and I... I saved this guy. It was a lot to process."

"You saved a guy?"

I nod. "Everyone was drunk, including him. I remembered a video I watched on CPR, and, well, I just did it. It's why Cole is angry with me."

"Cole is angry you saved a boy's life?" Dad questions with his brows furrowing. "I don't understand."

"His pride is hurt, I guess. I had to perform mouth-to-mouth. Kids at school were teasing Cole that I cheated on him."

Dad finally nods as it all makes sense. "Alexa, you should never be made to feel like saving a person's life is wrong."

"I know," I mumble. "I'm sorry, Dad."

A heavy sigh escapes him. "I'm not going to stop you from going to Europe, Alexa. Only if you promise me you will enroll when you return. A college education is integral to your future. Do you understand me?"

With my posture falling like the weight of the world is on my shoulders, I exhale a long breath trying to remain strong.

A year will give me plenty of time to explore and do all the things I want to do. Now with Cole gone, I'm no longer forced to consider someone else's fragile ego. The last thing I want right now is a guy telling me what I can or can't do. The whole jealousy thing is a bunch of BS. I don't understand men. It's not sexy at all.

Cole may have been my first love, but he won't be my last.

Just like Mom once told me, your first love will hurt the most. It'll be the one you remember, but maybe one day, it will also be the one that guides your heart in the right direction.

Mine is desperate to get on a plane to escape as far away as possible.

And in just under three months, my so-called broken heart and I will be doing exactly that.

FOUR

"Damn, you're old."

Ava raises a toast as the rest of my family follows. Given I'm not allowed to drink legally, the mocktail is at least pretty in color, with strawberries floating on top and cotton candy hovering to the side. It's sweet and lacks the main ingredient called *alcohol*.

"You wish you were still eighteen," I counter with a grin, taking a small sip to avoid a sugar rush. "You're old."

My family is known to throw extravagant parties when it comes to big milestones. Correction, I say my family when I mean Ava. With everything happening of late, I begged her not to throw a party. I'm just not in the mood. It was only last week I broke up with Cole, and it's been harder than I thought to be single again. Maybe it's because we share some classes or because our lockers are right next to each other. He knew I hated cafeteria food, so he would make sure he brought me food I would actually eat.

It's just the small things that all became one big thing. I relied on him for so long, not even realizing just how much. Not having a safety net of a boyfriend feels very lonesome.

I thought I was doing better yesterday until Krissy, another senior, made sure to throw herself all over Cole at his locker. It's not like he kissed her, but he didn't stop her either when she ran her hands inside his jacket.

It was enough to make me turn around, exit the building in a rush, and cry to myself inside my car in the parking lot, where no one could hear me. Then, I had to go home, deal with my parents, and pretend everything was okay.

As for turning eighteen, I gave Ava strict instructions on a small, intimate dinner. It ended up being just my sisters and parents. Will was stuck in Boston after the airport was shut down a few hours ago because of some gas leak. Austin got called into an emergency at the hospital. Addy's fiancé, Masen, sprained his ankle playing football with his brother yesterday and is on crutches. He offered to come, but I suggested he stay home, given that planes and crutches aren't the best combinations.

Thankfully, Millie and Ava organized babysitters because their kids are too crazy. It's like a damn zoo every time they're all together, the noise combined with the constant running around. If it's not that, it's the questions and stupid facts about games or kids' stuff I don't care about.

"Now, girls," Dad intervenes with his whisky in hand. "If anyone's old, it's me."

Millie places her hand on Dad's shoulder as Mom hides her smile behind her napkin. I'm admiring her white blazer with the large gold buttons. She's wearing it with a black-laced bodysuit underneath and high-waisted jeans. Of all us sisters, Ava is exactly my size which is why I raid her wardrobe often. Millie has a different style, though I have to admit she's beautiful and can pull anything off. We joke she has curves in the right places but learned our lesson not to say that in front of Will anymore without it turning into something dirty.

"According to the internet and the many social media accounts dedicated to you…" Ava continues while trying to hold back her laughter, "… age ain't nothing but a number."

Addy shakes her head in disgust. "It should be age ain't nothing but a bank account. The mentality of young girls these days astounds me."

"You mean the whole hooking up with an older man?" Ava questions and then digs her fork into the salad she's eating. "I mean, what's really considered too old?"

"Hmm, it depends where you are in life, I guess," Mom adds, raising her cocktail glass which appears almost empty. This better not be one of those times when she gets drunk or I'm wearing my headphones because hearing her giggle in the bedroom is just traumatizing.

"Okay, well, I think ten years is safe," Millie says.

"Of course, you have to say that." Ava purses her lips before rolling her eyes. "Will is ten years older than you."

Millie juts her chin with a dismissive glance. "And? I'm just saying it's normal these days."

This conversation is grossing me out. Older men? I could barely manage someone my age. An older man would be demanding in the bedroom, or maybe that is all men.

"I have a client who is sixty-seven, and he's married to a twenty-five-year-old," Addy tells us.

"Ew," I say in unison with Ava. "That's gross."

"Maybe they love each other," Millie suggests but then shakes her head. "Okay, but how old does he look? If he looks like he's in his forties, then it's not bad. Does he need help walking?"

"Can he even get it up?" Ava asks.

Dad bows his head and then covers his face with his hands. "Ava, do you have to?"

"Sorry, Dad, but Viagra can only get you so far. I'm not saying all old men need it, but..." Ava's eyes widen then she chases down a glass of wine. "God, someone save me now..."

"Girls." Mom chuckles softly. "Love is love and sex is sex. Depends on what's important to you. Now, can we get back to celebrating my baby's birthday?"

The cake coming out is a welcoming distraction from Ava veering onto Viagra talk in front of Dad. Everyone sings happy birthday before I'm requested to make a wish.

A wish, huh?

I wish for a new life. To be happy doing what I want to do without living up to everyone's expectations.

But of all the wishes I could wish for at this moment, it's to make all the nightmares disappear.

The candles burn bright before I lean forward and blow them out one by one. My family claps and cheer, as I glance at everyone at the table, I wonder how being part of this family can be a blessing and burden all at the same time.

Millie and Ava are the first to leave since they have babysitters at home and need to get back early. Ava promises me a shopping day out which is hit or miss depending on her mood. Sometimes, her taste is on point. Other times, I wonder what the hell she thinks about making me try on some old-lady dress. It ends up with us arguing, which is why we always take separate cars.

Addy is flying back home tomorrow, so I welcome her stay since it was just her and I living with my parents for the longest time.

Back at home, as predicted, Mom did drink too much. She starts giggling, her steps wobbly as she attempts the stairs. Dad wraps his hand around her waist to help but then leans in to whisper. Whatever he says makes her giggle louder. I can't believe these two are so inappropriate as if Addy and I are invisible tonight.

"Can you believe these two?" I complain aloud to Addy. "After being married for this long, why do they still act like horny teenagers?"

Addy laughs, lacing her arm into mine, and walks us to the patio outside. It's a beautiful night out, warm but not uncomfortable. I'm so full from dinner and the mocktails, so the idea of lying by the pool feels perfect.

We both lay down, removing our shoes and glancing at the sky.

"You know, most women envy what Mom and Dad have," Addy says wistfully.

"What do they have?"

"Unconditional love, comfort, connection, and a friendship," she begins with, then continues. "A lot of women I see are still searching for all of this. It's not easy to find someone who is equally your partner and best friend plus have sexual chemistry at the same time."

"What do you mean sexual chemistry?"

"It just works. There are no boundaries, no rules. Everything is from within, and when you're at a level of comfort with a partner, it's a freedom like no other."

"That makes no sense to me," I admit truthfully. "There are always rules. Like, don't cheat on me."

Addy chuckles softly. "Sure, if you're not in an open relationship. Those rules are kind of a given, though. Once you commit to someone, you trust them unless, of course, they give you reason not to trust them, but that's a whole other story."

My mind wanders back to Cole and me. While I don't think Cole cheated on me, we often fought when rumors swirled around school about him hooking up with other girls. I'm not proud of moments when our fights escalated and we would get into a screaming match. Equally so, he hated it when any guy went near me.

What Addy said about love, comfort, and connection doesn't sound anything like what Cole and I had. It then gets me started on 'what did we have?'

"You're quiet," Addy points out.

"Just thinking about what you said."

"You and Cole?"

"Yeah."

"Alexa, you're young. Don't settle for a high school boyfriend if it doesn't feel right."

I nod, in silence, shifting my gaze to the lights on the horizon.

"We're broken up. It's done. I didn't settle."

"Despite what everyone else thinks, I think it's a good idea you're traveling to find yourself."

My head tilts toward Addy. "I'm not traveling to find myself. I'm traveling to explore the world."

"Same thing, Alexa. We explore because we're searching for something."

Without even thinking, my mouth opens to correct her, but something stops me, and I keep quiet.

"Mom and Dad will support you no matter what," Addy continues. "That's what our parents do. Go explore and do whatever it is you want to do. As for college, it's next year's problem. Live for the now because tomorrow is not promised."

A small laugh escapes me. "Ava is right. Every chat with you is like a therapy session."

Addy shakes her head, then snorts. "If Ava were a client of mine, I'd be sitting on some nice coin if I could bill her.

Her trick is to call me and start the conversation with, 'I have a friend' The friend is always her."

I continue to laugh, knowing Ava too well. "That's Ava for you."

Addy clutches her stomach as we both fall into a fit of laughter, unable to control ourselves. I'm going to miss her. If there's anyone who has ever had my back, it's Addison Edwards.

Turning eighteen and graduating from high school flew past in the blink of an eye. I wasn't nervous about graduating. Just glad it was finally over. I'd managed to graduate with honors, even surprising myself with how my grades were excellent given what I'd been through the last few months.

All my family, including my aunts, uncles, and cousins, were at the ceremony. Many of them cried though I'm not sure why. I was just so relieved it was over, and I didn't have to see everyone in this godforsaken school anymore.

Initially, I planned to leave for Europe as soon as school was over. Then, I got a summer job opportunity making it hard to refuse. My mom's bestie, Eric, had a client who needed a house sitter for the summer. House is probably not the right word to use, more like mansion sitter. The mansion is located in Santa Barbara, and part of the job also involved dog-sitting the three King Charles Cavaliers—Paul, Ringo, and Adele.

The English couple who owns the place are traveling to Asia and would usually bring their dogs, but apparently, on the last trip, there was an incident with airport staff and Paul. He got snappy, and they got slapped with a big fine.

They paid extremely well, so well even Eric said I'd be a fool to pass it up.

"I would have died for a job like this when I was slaving away to make a dollar at your age," Eric complains, pouring himself a martini in the fancy bar inside the den.

"What were you doing at eighteen?"

"Street work," he answers flatly.

"Street work? Like a hooker or male equivalent?"

"God no," Eric exasperates, placing his hand on his chest. "Modeling on the streets for some D-grade fashion magazine."

My shoulders fall as I roll my eyes at him. "Okay, you can see how I took that wrong, right?"

"Sweetheart," he calls with a big grin. "Enjoy this while you can. Soon you'll be backpacking through Europe, questioning whether you can afford deodorant. Then, you decide food is more important, and it's a slippery slope from there on."

"Like you've ever done it." Ringo walks over to me and rests his head on my lap. Adele is not impressed as she lays on the dog bed but continues to give me the cold shoulder. Paul is standing at the window, eyeing the gardener with a wicked death stare. "You only stay in five-star hotels."

"The way God intended it," Eric responds with a smile. "According to my friend Harper, you'll need the following things. A hot girl bikini for the beach and pool. Stick to white. It's the best color against the European tan you'll have."

"Okay..."

"Black body-con mini dress. You can style it up with accessories that are light to carry," Eric rambles, barely taking a breath. "Now, even though I loathe flats with a mini, you'll want some sandals to go with it. Heels will not be your friend when you're drunk and trying to walk down a flight of steps in Santorini."

"Got it, sandals."

"And listen, just make sure you stay protected." Eric lets out a heavy sigh. "No glove, no love."

"C'mon," I joke, unable to keep a straight face. "As if I'd sleep with a stranger in a foreign country."

Eric places his hand on mine. His face turned serious. "Honey, we all do it. Most of us live to regret it unless, of course, it's some Italian man who can't speak English with a big dong which makes your eyes water."

"You fucked an Italian man with a big dong which made your eyes water?"

"Sweetheart, I couldn't walk straight for *weeks*."

All of a sudden, my ass begins to hurt. Eric has had a colorful past. Thank God he's married now because I just can't imagine him still on the loose. He talks a lot of smack for someone married, but Tristan, his husband, is used to his ways and pretty much ignores it.

"This conversation hurts," I tell him.

Most of our summer days were spent lounging by the pool. For someone with a full-time job, Eric sure had a lot of spare time on his hands. He used to work for Mom as her assistant. Then he moved into marketing. Now, he owns his own PR company and works with high-profile celebrities, which, according to him, is his dream job.

The days passed quickly as did my time in this summer job. I'd finished planning my itinerary for the next year, including a stop in all the countries I'm keen to visit.

Then, it came time to say goodbye. It's supposed to be easy, given my excitement. What I didn't expect was this wild ride of emotions. One minute I'm dreaming about lying by the pool in Mykonos. The next, I'm almost crying because I don't want to leave the house.

The morning of my departure is a quiet one. Mom made breakfast—pancakes and waffles—just how I like them mixed together. The fresh brew of coffee smells extra good, even though I'm not a coffee drinker unless Starbucks Iced Coffee counts.

Outside, the sun is extra bright today. The birds even seem to have an extra chirp in their chirping.

I pull on the zipper and close my backpack. Everything is packed and ready to go. As I throw the oversized backpack over my shoulder, I glance at my room one more time.

There are so many memories, good and bad. I wonder if the next time I see it, will it be different? Mom won't touch a thing, but will I feel different?

With a weight on my shoulders from the bag, not just my emotions, I close the door behind me and carefully make my way down the stairs. Inside the kitchen, my parents glance at me with sadness in their eyes.

"Do you have your passport?" Mom asks quietly.

I throw my backpack on the ground and retrieve the passport from the crossbody bag I'm also wearing. Holding it up, Mom nods with a small smile.

"We haven't discussed money," Dad begins, his voice suddenly stiff and controlled. "The limit on your credit card has been increased to pay for accommodations and in case of emergency."

"About that..." I reach inside my bag again and pull out my credit card. Before I have a chance to talk myself out of it, I place it flat on the countertop. "I won't be needing it."

"Alexa," Mom calls my name with worry. "I'd be much more at ease if you kept it. You don't need to use it, but just for emergencies."

I shake my head, refusing to compromise. If I do this, I need to do this on my own. My gaze shifts toward Dad. I can swear on everything I own, somewhere behind his challenging stare, there is a bit of him which is proud I'm not leeching off him like Ava.

"I'll be fine, Mom. Don't worry."

Mom bites her lip, then bows her head. "You're our baby. We'll always worry about you."

Taking a step toward where she stands, I reach my arms out to embrace her. Mom's hug is extra tight today, and I know she doesn't want me to grow up, but it's not like I can stay young forever.

"You'll see me in four months at Addy's wedding in France," I remind her.

A smile finally spreads across her face. "We're here, always. Just a call away."

"I know, Mom."

Finally, I turn to face Dad. The moment is finally here, the moment I'd been wishing for every single time we argued, and he imposed a stupid new rule.

In my head, I thought I'd be jumping for joy. Reality feels incredibly different... like I'm going to miss him or something.

"I guess this is it..."

"This is what you wanted," he reminds me in a condescending tone.

My eyes meet his, and perhaps his words were intended one way, but, to me, he just sounded like a jerk again. A swirl of anger begins to swell inside me. I try to suppress it, knowing nothing good will come from arguing with him again. I swear he's like a woman on her period with his up-and-down moods.

"Bye, Dad."

I wrap my arms around him to say goodbye, but unexpectedly, he holds on longer than I anticipated. When I finally pull away, Mom's eyes are glassy as she tries to hold back her tears.

"Are you sure you don't want us to take you to the airport?" Mom asks for the millionth time.

"I got this, Mom. Like I said, I'll be just fine..."

FIVE

"Alexandra, you wanna move a little faster?"

I bite my tongue, then wipe the sweat off my forehead, ignoring his thick accent which has escalated to yelling from the kitchen. I should be grateful he at least spoke to me in English because he usually barks orders in French, making it hard for me to catch everything without asking someone for help.

Weeknights weren't usually this busy, but some soccer game finished, and fans wanted to celebrate. They entered the bar in droves, ecstatic over their win. We are short-staffed, and I was supposed to end this shift two hours ago. My plan was to go back to the room I'd been renting for the last month and get some sleep before catching a train out to Champagne tomorrow to see my family.

Everyone is flying in for Masen and Addy's wedding. As I agreed to be a bridesmaid at the wedding, there's no way I can miss it. I don't exactly want to show up with bags under my eyes from the back-to-back shifts I pulled this week. It'll give my sisters ammunition to lecture me with

this   whole   life-ain't-so-easy-without-Daddy's-money
speech.

Boy, I know it. I'm so exhausted I could fall asleep right
here in the middle of this busy bar. The struggle is *real*.

It's been four months since I left home for the trip of a
lifetime. Okay, sure, there have been some fun moments if
you ignore the whole being responsible and working thing.

In the months which have passed, I've worked three
different jobs. The first was at a small café in London. I did
pretty well for my first job abroad, considering I'd never
made coffee in my life. It didn't take me long to pick up, and
by the time I moved to Italy, I enjoyed drinking coffee,
having smelled it all day long.

Italy was much harder to navigate, given I didn't speak
Italian and relied on my phone to translate. For the first
time since I left the States, I began to feel homesick. Everything felt completely different, and communicating with
people was so hard. Some days, I just gave up in frustration
and retreated to the small room I shared with three other
girls. Two of them were from the East Coast and the other
was from New Zealand.

They were nice enough to hang out with. We spent a
week together sightseeing, then found ourselves a good-
paying job at a restaurant in Milan. Given we were kitchen
hands, it wasn't exciting or life-changing, just enough
money to take us on our next adventure.

I promised to meet up with them in Greece next month,
once I'm done with my time in France.

"Alexandra, *vite*!"

The manager yells at me to hurry. By the end of the
shift, I could barely move my legs, and I smelled of grease,
among other things. Eric was so right when he said you get
to a point when you question your need for deodorant

because of the desire to eat a decent meal. I thought about it, but the idea of working up a sweat unprotected didn't sit right with me. So, I wasn't eating fancy-ass healthy meals, big deal.

I slept like a baby, only barely making it to the train station in time. With all my items safely with me, the train ride is supposed to take just under two hours.

As the train pulled out of the station, I found myself staring out the window, deciding not to fall asleep in case I missed my stop. If there's anything I'm looking forward to, it's the big comfortable beds at my parents' château. Also, showering without a time limit and wondering if some perverted person is peeping through the makeshift peephole I found once in the bathroom.

It's funny how your mind can just drift for hours on end. Before I know it, my stop is next. Mom said she would pick me up at the station since my sisters were busy and Dad was at some winery he owns doing business, of course.

When the train stops, I see Mom waving on the platform. She looks exactly the same, maybe even younger, if that's possible. Her mousy brown hair has grown out a little, and she looks fantastic in the camel-colored maxi dress she's wearing. Maybe I should have worn something more fun besides my denim shorts and boring old white tank, but most of the clothes inside my backpack are dirty since I was too busy to hit the laundromat this week.

My heart races as I find myself running off the train and into her arms. The moment she embraces me, her familiar smell feels just like *home*.

"I missed you, kid."

I hold onto her tight. "Missed you, Mom."

She pulls back to examine me better. Her brows draw

together into a worried expression. Here we go, a lecture is just about to come out of her mouth.

"Oh, Alexa, have you been eating?"

"Yes, Mom." I huff with an eye roll. "I've just been on my feet more."

"Okay, okay," Mom says while motioning me to follow her to the car. "I've got four days to enjoy you and make sure you eat."

The drive through the countryside is relaxing. Mom and I texted almost daily, but it's nice to hear her complain about my sisters in person.

"Addy is a dream bride," Mom begins with, then continues. "Is it possible for Eric to be a bridezilla even though he's not the one getting married?"

"Hmm... I think that's just called Ericzilla."

Mom laughs. "I dare you to call him that to his face."

"I'm sure someone will." I chuckle.

The familiar stone château appears on my right. Mom takes the turn into the long driveway lined with trees. As a child, I loved visiting and would often pretend I was Rapunzel trapped in the tower waiting for my prince. I can't help but laugh. Who the hell wants to wait for a man, and what about all the split ends having to maintain such long hair? I swear fairy tales are so impractical and pathetic.

After Mom parks the car, a black Mercedes pulls up behind us. When the dust settles, the door opens, and my father steps out wearing a gray suit. It's a little less formal, given he's wearing no tie. His tall stature stands out as he glances at me with a small smile. Like Mom, he appears to look younger. What is with these two? Maybe with me gone, there's less stress, and they're probably having the time of their lives.

Don't even go where you're about to go.

His expression doesn't look welcoming. I don't even get a big I-miss-you greeting as I did with Mom. Ignoring the unsettling feeling inside my chest, I remember who I'm dealing with.

"Alexa," he voices in a low tone. "I'm glad you could join us."

He opens his arms, and even though I reluctantly go in for the hug, his aftershave reminds me of all the times he held me as a child. The times I fell over and cried to when I just wanted to sit in his lap for his attention because my sisters weren't around.

I pull back, not wanting to get all nostalgic, lingering too long already. "Nice to see you, Dad."

Mom purses her lips, almost annoyed with him, but he ignores her and turns his back to enter the house. I bow my head for Mom to place her hand on my shoulder. It shouldn't have hurt, seeing him ignore me like I'm a nobody, but the pang in my heart argues it does.

"He hasn't been doing well since you left. Don't be fooled by his stubborn exterior. You know him well. It takes him a while to adjust to things."

My mouth remains closed since there's no point in arguing. Been there, done that.

Lex Edwards is being typical Lex Edwards.

We enter the château through the large wooden arched doors. The noise from the chatter and laughs is the first thing I hear. All my sisters and their families are sitting around the living room. The kids are the first to greet me, running toward me and grabbing my legs because that's all they can reach. I throw my bags on the floor, leaning down to hug each one of them.

"Auntie Alexa," Archer calls while squashing his little face. "You look funny."

Great—nice greeting, kid.

"Archer, that's not nice," Ashton scolds his little brother. "Daddy says you must always compliment a woman, especially if you want someone."

I purse my lips, trying to hold back my smile. "Is that what Daddy said? It sounds to me like Daddy is often in the doghouse."

"A doghouse?" Archer questions then laughs. "Daddy doesn't fit in our doghouse!"

My hands reach out to ruffle Archer's mousy brown hair. Will and Millie's sons have grown so much. They're talking a mile a minute, but I hear the word *Pokémon* come up, and I'm tuning out.

Their youngest son, Alexander, takes steps but is unsteady on his feet. He's so chubby I just want to eat him from the cheeks to those thighs. I reach my arms out to cuddle him, but his face breaks into a loud cry. I have never felt more attacked by stranger danger than I have right now. Way to go, chubby.

Ava's daughter, Emmy, is standing on my left like a little princess in her purple tutu. I reach down to grab her, swinging her in my arms. She looks exactly like Ava, it's crazy. Ava's youngest daughter, River, is asleep in the stroller which is sitting in the corner of the room. She looks more like Austin, two very different-looking sisters.

"Aunty Alexa, when are you coming home?" she asks so innocently before resting her head on my shoulder.

I move a strand of hair away from her face and ignore the tightness inside my chest. The idea of traveling to gain some freedom from my parents was great until the reality of who else I left behind begins to sink in.

"Soon, I promise."

Will is next to greet me, surprisingly dressed so casually.

He's usually in a suit and out with Dad doing billionaire business.

"What is this? Will Romano enjoying a holiday and not working for once?" I tease.

His forced smile turns into annoyance. "I've been instructed to relax which means no business."

I can't help but laugh. "It's hurting you, I can see."

"If Lex is allowed to work, why can't I?"

"I dunno, sounds like you're pussy-whipped. It's what happens when you marry those needy young girls."

Will chuckles then hugs me. "Good to see you, sis."

A nervous-looking Masen joins us. For someone getting married tomorrow, I guess it's expected, but I find it amusing given he's always been a cocky bastard, and for once, he looks like a wreck.

"You okay? You look nervous."

Masen pulls back with a grin. "Your family is a lot."

"Trust me, I know."

Ava jumps off the sofa, wearing a short denim jumpsuit that would look great on me in Greece. *Note—raid her room later*.

"Well, well, well," Ava says with a smirk on her face. "Look who's at a family event for once. And stop eyeing my jumpsuit. If you really want it, you can have it."

I go in for a hug, and she squeezes me super tight until I can't breathe.

"Ava..." I choke, "...you're squashing me, and yes, I do want your jumpsuit."

She finally lets go. "You're too skinny. Have you been eating at all?"

"Yes, but unlike your travel vlogs, I don't sit around all day by the pool drinking margaritas. Some of us must work."

Ava pinches my cheek with a wide smile. "Oh, poor baby is doing it tough?"

"Leave her alone," Austin scolds, then leans in for a quick embrace. "Ava makes you think it's margaritas, but it's mocktails because the girls are with us, and we learned our lesson the last time we got drunk on vacation."

"Oh, what happened?"

"Just kids being kids. Wake up at dawn. Hangovers and young children don't mix."

"Right." I nod with a grin. "So, what you're trying to say is Ava fakes it?"

"Hey!" Ava pouts but is distracted by Emmy asking for a snack.

Austin cocks his head with a smile. "You know your sister very well."

"Uh, my turn now," Millie interrupts, placing her arms around me. "You look different, mature perhaps."

"Can I take that as a compliment? Mom and Ava said I look skinny, but it was accompanied by a frown."

Millie's lips curve upward into a smile. "Sure. Why don't we go check on Addy? She's upstairs trying on her dress again."

We head upstairs quickly to avoid Ava following since she'll nag me again about what I've been doing. Down the long hall is a bunch of rooms with Addy's on the far left. Millie knocks softly, then we both enter.

Addy is standing in front of the mirror, absolutely stunning in the open-back laced dress she wears. The design itself is simple but so elegant and timeless. I've never seen my sister look so beautiful. Her bronze-colored hair flows down her back, much longer than I remember and lighter too.

"So, what do you think?" Addy asks with a big smile on

her face. "I'm so happy you're here, little sister. You look well-traveled."

"I think you look beautiful and not nervous like your soon-to-be husband," I tell her, then hug her carefully not to ruin the dress. "Are you nervous, though?"

Addy shakes her head. "Nah, I love him, and it's just our family."

After one more glance in the mirror, Addy extends her hands to reach out for mine. There's a twinkle in her eyes, some might call it love, I suppose. My sister looks happy, and that makes me happy to see her finally say I do with the man she loves.

"The ceremony will be over before you know it. Soon you'll be Mrs. Cooper." Millie grins.

Addy squeezes my hand tight then squeals as Millie and I both laugh.

"I love the sound of that."

SIX

The rehearsal dinner is *chaos*.

I thought last night's so-called relaxed dinner was chaotic, but now the rest of the family has arrived, this is chaos-chaos.

My Uncle Noah and Aunt Kate, plus my cousins Nash and Sienna were the first to arrive. I'm pretty sure Nash only came to hook up with some French chicks since he only cares about his dick. He once told us the only reason he went to USC is because he read somewhere it rated the best college with the hottest chicks. I don't know what forum he read that on, but chances are there was no merit or studies behind it.

Sienna had recently moved to Manhattan to pursue her modeling career, much to Uncle Noah's disapproval. I remember when Uncle Noah showed up to our house late one night trying to convince Mom to talk some sense into Aunt Kate for allowing Sienna to model. At the time, it wasn't anything major until she started getting more noticed. Sienna told us in our group chat that when she mentioned Victoria's Secret to him, he almost disowned her.

He's so much like Dad—arrogant, close-minded, and so controlling with his daughters.

They have their own château next door, and staying with them are my Aunt Adriana and Uncle Julian, along with my cousins Luna and Willow. The place is big enough for everyone, thank God. Our place feels like a nuthouse with all the crazy kids running around.

Eric, of course, came with Tristan. They are staying in some place in town which Ava thinks is a French swingers club. I chose not to ask, given I wanted to keep my dinner down. Of course, she went on and on about swinging which, in my opinion, she knew way too much.

Masen's parents, Haden and Presley, were also staying close by with their son Cruz, Addy's bestie. To be honest, I'm surprised he came, but according to Ava, all is well in their friendship. There was a time when Cruz was in love with Addy, but then she went sneaking around with Masen. Talk about complicated.

I often wonder how Ava manages to get anything done since she's up in everyone's business. Who needs TMZ when you have an older sister like Ava?

My cousins, Andy and Jessa, though it's still weird to call them a married couple when, in fact, they are both my cousins but on either side of the family, we're the only ones unable to make it. Jessa is in her last trimester and unable to fly. Millie did promise to make sure we video call the whole event so they can be there in real-time.

The last to arrive are Rocky and Nikki, Will's parents, with his younger brother, Beau. They took a late flight in from JFK which explains why they look wrecked and are also staying somewhere in town.

Beau is another person I'm surprised to see. Much like me, he rarely attends family events, always trying to find an excuse or is probably busy with the string of girls he leads on. I'm assuming his parents dragged him here against his will.

The dinner is being held at a local vineyard, the one Dad and Uncle Noah co-own, or something like that. The restaurant located on the property is cozy but enough to fit a long wooden table with seats for everyone. There are candles everywhere, but thankfully the kids are smart enough not to touch them. At least, the older ones are. Ava's daughter, River, has been eyeing them for a solid ten minutes. With a pacifier in her mouth, she looks ready to strike at any moment and stick her chubby little hands out to touch them.

As I said, it's nothing but chaos. The kids are loud. The chatter is loud. Servers are weaving in and out, making sure everyone has a plate and glasses filled with wine. There's cheese everywhere. I saw some escargot, but that's a hard pass for me. If it comes down to snails or brains, I might just choose brains since I accidentally ordered it last week thinking it was veal.

There's lots of laughter and smiles, then a small toast as Ava mentioned the big toast is for tomorrow night. I don't understand why we are having a pre-wedding dinner, given tomorrow's reception will be the same thing with the same people.

This is what happens when your father is a billionaire. Money to burn like it's nothing. Meanwhile, I've been busting my ass just to survive. *Don't complain. You chose not to accept his money.*

After dinner, I take a quick walk around the grounds just to burn off the food since I'm not used to eating so much anymore. I'm not sure whether it was all the cheese or whatever meat I ate, but something isn't sitting right.

The air is crisp and clean, nothing at all like the air back home. When I cross a small footbridge back toward the main area, I turn a corner and bump into a hard body.

"Oh God," I yell, startled by the encounter as my heart races. Quickly, I look up to see it's Beau. "Shit, Beau? You scared me."

His hand grips my arms as he holds me in place while I try to calm down. My breaths begin to slow, but my heart is still thumping loudly.

"I'm surprised you remember me." Beau releases his grip from my arms, but his piercing hazel eyes continue to stare at me. "Aren't you a woman of the world now? The rebel going against Daddy's wishes?"

The fancy champagne is sitting on the tall tables scattered across the patio. I motion for him to follow me, so I can grab a glass. With the drink in hand, I down it in one go, then place it back down.

My insides turn warm and fuzzy, which is oddly satisfying. Only now, I take a proper look at Beau. When did he get so tall? Maybe it's the dark suit. Usually, he's dressed so casually in a tee and jeans. My eyes wander to the tattoo on his neck, then the other on his hand. I want to ask out of curiosity, but in the same breath, I don't want him to think I was looking at him in any other way than a family member attending my sister's wedding.

From what I last heard, he's still bumming in Manhattan with his parents. Perhaps *bumming* is the wrong word since their apartment is on Park Avenue and Beau attended some private school. According to the various gossip channels in my family, Beau is a notorious trouble-maker unlike his billionaire older brother.

"And what are you doing with your life, huh?" I ask, staring at him fiercely. "Looking for your next target? As long as she can spread her legs, right? Isn't that what boys your age want?"

"Boys?" he questions with a raised brow. "Quite the chip on your shoulder, Miss Edwards. What happened to the good little girl who would play nice with me when our parents insisted we hang out? Who hurt you, huh?"

"I'm not a little girl anymore," I drag, not wanting to answer him. "Anyway, I'm surprised you're here."

"How can I pass up an opportunity to drink champagne in Champagne? I'm nineteen... makes it all legal here."

I glance around, watching my family busy themselves in chit-chat. No one saw me take a glass, and given the legal drinking age is eighteen, I reach for another two, then hand Beau one. His crooked smile turns into a mischievous grin before he downs the contents of the glass in one go.

"The perks of being in Europe," I say with a smile. "Freedom to live life to the fullest."

"The last I heard, you've been waiting tables at some seedy pub in London," he answers in a condescending tone. "Hope that's all you're doing to make cash."

I purse my lips. "You've been misinformed. The café was great in London. The place in Italy was, let's say, uneventful. The bar in Paris... I'm just glad it was only a week. As for you insinuating I make money with my body, you're a jerk for even thinking that."

"Now, now," he teases, cocking his head. "Play nice, Alexa."

My shoulders remain straight, not wanting him to think I'm having a horrible time since he might blab it to someone in my family. It wasn't *that* bad. Sure, it's not glamorous, but it's not like I can go back home and have my father tell me he was right, or even worse, borrow money in which Ava is right.

I hate it when Ava is right.

"So, then what I heard isn't all true?"

"What else have you heard?"

Beau shrugs, but his eyes tell a different story. "You're not going to college. You broke up with your boyfriend."

"Is Millie telling you all this?" I ask, then sigh. "I mean, whatever, so I'm single, and college is... it's not on my mind."

"You're young and beautiful. Just stay single. As for college, it ain't so bad."

His words stir a weird sensation in my stomach, close to a flutter. For a brief moment, I glance up, then look away. Of course, Beau enjoys college. He's probably slept with all of the sorority house by now. I have no idea where he goes or what he plans to major in. Frankly, I've no desire to ask. The least of my favorite topics is college.

My heart races, but the feeling quickly subsides as I realize just how desperate I am if a comment from Beau can make me feel a certain way. He's Will's brother, end of story. There hasn't been a guy since Cole, and maybe I need a fling of some sort to get it out of my system.

God, if only Eric could hear my internal thoughts. He'd be rejoicing and telling me just how proud he is.

Oh, and no glove, no love.

I shudder at the thought.

"We should probably get back and hang with the family."

Beau nods with a smirk but remains quiet. I'm waiting for him to say something that will most likely annoy me, something he's done since we were kids. We were the youngest kids in our families, therefore our parents dumped us together. That, and our siblings were too cool to hang out with us.

But Beau has always been one to watch out for.

Three... two... one.

"You go back. Nash and I are heading out."

"Out?" I question, crossing my arms. "We're in the middle of nowhere."

He rubs his chin, glancing at Nash, who is eyeing him to hurry up. Nash is just as bad with his women, barely able to hold a girlfriend. Every time I see him, there's someone new.

"There's a place in town suited for gentlemen."

I shake my head in disgust. "Gross, how sleazy of you."

Beau chuckles but then reaches out to touch my arm. "The players gotta play, right?"

With those words said, he leaves me standing alone to meet with Nash. Men are so... *argh.* How are you supposed to be attracted to them or even consider committing for a lifetime when all they want is pussy?

There—I said it, and I'm calling bullshit.

Or maybe I'm drunk from two glasses of champagne.

Either way, Beau has put me in a bad mood.

And tomorrow, I'm supposed to be a proud bridesmaid walking down the aisle supporting the act of love.

More champagne... definitely more champagne.

SEVEN

"I now pronounce you husband and wife. You may kiss the bride."

Masen reaches out to cup Addy's face and slowly draws her close before planting a soft yet non-pornographic kiss in front of everyone. Thank God, you never know how these kisses are supposed to turn out.

There's loud cheering and clapping, plus an obnoxious whistle that had to come from Rocky. His suit is incredibly tight, something Eric has been giving him heat about all day. I briefly overheard the argument and how Rocky assumed he could fit into the same suit he wore to Will and Millie's wedding. Turns out, he couldn't.

I stand alongside my sisters, all of us wearing pale blue dresses, though thankfully not matching. Ava did well with the choices, respecting our personal tastes yet thinking of Addy as well. Mine is an off-the-shoulder dress that sits just above my knee. She paired it with simple gold strappy heels, nothing over-the-top to keep everything elegant.

My parents watched on proudly from the front, as did Masen's parents. It's still hard to believe Masen and Addy just got married, given how much they despised each other. If I had to call it, I honestly thought it would be Addy and Cruz, given they were so close for the longest time.

I glance over at Cruz, who appears to be in good spirits. I'm glad he didn't pull a dramatic move like stopping the wedding. You never know what someone may do if they're still in love with a person they can't have.

The newlyweds hold hands to walk down the small aisle. The wedding is being held in the same vineyard we went to last night. Only this time, the table is set outside in the large open area which overlooks the winery. Fairy lights line the wooden planks above the outdoor area everywhere you look. They're mixed and wrapped around the vines, which hang to create an inviting ambiance. It's crazy pretty, and if I admit to myself, romantic to the point I actually miss having a boyfriend.

The sun is soon to set, but everyone makes their way to the pre-drinks area before dinner is served.

"Thank God that went off without any trouble." Eric lets out a relieved sigh beside me. His Fendi suit is also pale blue, matching our dresses. "You never know what can happen."

"Nothing was going to happen," I tell him while side-eyeing Ava. "Masen and Addy love each other."

"Excuse me?" Eric raises his tone with a serious expression. "Are we forgetting about the complicated besties' love triangle saga?"

"There was no saga," Ava drags. "There was a misunderstanding or perhaps mixed feelings. A saga would refer to a long dramatic love affair like—"

"Lex and Charlie," Eric interrupts.

Mom stops walking and turns to face us. "Hey, what did you say about me?"

Eric puts on a fake smile. "Oh, nothing, doll. Just reminiscing about your wondrous love story."

Annoyed, Mom purses her lips and then turns back around to ignore Eric.

"Phew," Eric whispers. "Don't rile the beast. She's got her period and is pissed she can't fuck Daddy in the big château.

Ava and I groan in unison, and then my hand reaches out to slap his arm. "I need therapy now. Don't ever say the D word again."

Eric raises his brows, then lets out an obnoxious laugh. "Honey, a leopard can't change its spots."

"The leopard can learn to at least shut its goddamn mouth," Ava reprimands.

My eyes shift to Addy, who finishes talking to Aunt Adriana. Quickly excusing myself with a desperate need to forget about Eric's loose mouth, I make my way over and give her the biggest of hugs.

"I can't believe you did it!"

Addy raises her hand to show off her gorgeous diamond wedding band, waving it proudly. "I'm a wife!"

"So, Addison Cooper, huh? Or are you going to copy Millie and Ava? Do the whole Edwards hyphenated thing as well?"

"Kinda hard since Masen's name is technically Masen Malone-Cooper," Addy informs me. "That would make me Addison Edwards Malone-Cooper."

Masen wraps his arms around Addy, then gently places his lips on her shoulder to leave a soft kiss. I'm not a romantic person by nature, but that right there was a romantic move.

I take a deep breath, my mind drifting back to the times

I'd spent with Cole. It wasn't long ago, months even, but it sure felt like a lifetime.

When we first started flirting in class, it was the thrill of the chase. Every girl wanted him, but he had his eyes set on me. It went on for weeks at the beginning of my senior year until he finally asked me out.

It wasn't long before things got hot and heavy. Cole wasn't a virgin, but I was. I tried to wait as long as possible, but things got more intense each time we were alone. He always wanted more, and my body started to feel the same. The first time we had sex, it wasn't great. Uncomfortable, actually. He promised me it would get better, and it did as time went on.

I guess it was just hard to juggle his demands as well as school, plus a controlling father.

It's not like Cole wasn't romantic at times. He did have a good side to him. Things just moved too fast and too soon.

Then, I found out I was pregnant.

"Alexa," my name is called by Aunt Adriana. "Away with the fairies?"

"Huh, is that another old-person saying?"

Aunt Adriana presses her lips together with a judging stare. "I'm not old. I'll have you know I'm still as active as the day I turned twenty-one. Though maybe a sore lower back, but who doesn't have a sore back these days?"

"Me." Eric has to insert himself into the conversation. He's known to have major FOMO. "And I'll tell you why. The key to avoiding back problems is to make sure you do the right exercises. For example, you'll want to be bent over in a comfortable position."

I raise my hand. "I'm out."

For the second time today—actually third, if you

counted his ramble about pegging when we were trying to zip Millie's dress past her ass—I'm walking away from Eric.

In desperate need of something to drink, I make my way to grab champagne. It's all I've drunk in the last day, and I'm surprised the multiple glasses last night didn't leave me with a hangover. The endless conversations last night with everyone asking me the same questions made it a long night. *When are you coming home? What college will you attend once you're back?* Blah, blah, blah.

"So, drinking again?"

I turn around to see Beau standing behind me. With a drink in his hand that looks like a bourbon, he looks extra handsome in his gray suit. Again, nothing like the guy I remember who would torment me in the cubby house and insist an earthquake was coming leading to our morbid deaths.

A typical East Coast boy who *hated* California.

His dark brown hair is kind of messy, probably because I've seen him run his hands through it multiple times. Only now do I notice the tattoo on the side of his neck appears to be an image of something. I can't work out exactly what it is without getting closer. Then, my eyes gravitate to his hand, where I remember he has another. This tattoo appears to be script, but again, I can't figure out what without getting closer.

"Special occasion," I respond with a forced smile. "We have to celebrate the newlyweds."

"I guess you have a point." He extends his glass to clink. "Cheers."

Our glasses touch, then I take a sip, only to remember our conversation last night.

"So, how was your trip to the gentlemen's club last night? Catch any diseases?"

A smirk spreads across his face before he brings the glass to his lips. "Maybe, from the dirty restroom."

My face pulls back in disgust. "You fucked a whore in a public restroom?"

"Who said anything about a whore?"

"You did." My voice comes out all high-pitched like I'm annoyed or something. I take a breath to calm myself down. "You said you were going to a gentlemen's club."

"Yes, it was a gentlemen's club. The gentleman drank scotch and played poker," he informs me smugly. "You assumed it involved women."

My brows snap together as my lips press tightly while I glance at the ground, kicking a loose pebble.

"Oh, my bad."

"Do you really think I'm that type of guy? You're so hung up on me being a player."

Only now do I notice my dad watching us. His expression is soft. Even from a distance, his eyes shine bright in the emerald green he is known for. I quickly turn away, knowing his happiness is because of Addy, not me.

"I'm not into men," I blurt out, half thinking. "I mean, whatever. Do whatever you want."

"What happened? Got some girl-on-girl action during your time away?"

"What?" I shake my head. "No. That is such a guy thing to say. I meant to say I haven't thought about a guy for such a long time. It's kind of a nice thing sometimes to not have to worry about a boyfriend and just do my own thing."

Beau's smile is undeniable as he tilts his head with curiosity. "Let's see how long that will last."

I raise the glass of champagne to my lips. "Is it a bet or something? Because I could use the money."

Laughter escapes him. "What do you think? I'm some billionaire or something? Wrong brother."

We're interrupted as servers enter the space with trays of hors d'oeuvres. Just as I'm about to grab something to eat, Ava pulls me away to take photos with our family. The photographer is someone known in the fashion world though I didn't quite pick up his name given he sputtered in French. His demands, however, were intense.

Ava knows all her angles and where to place her hands and arms. I'm like a baby deer in the woods. Unless the camera is forward-facing in my hand in selfie mode, I have no clue how to pose.

The photographer took every combo possible, then started inviting the rest of the family. It dragged on forever. For the group shot, he strategically placed people based on height and who looked good next to who. There were a lot of couples but also a lot of us singles.

He directs Beau to stand behind me, with my cousin Luna on my other side. Something about us looked aesthetically pleasing together. I keep my smile fixed, despite my cousins teasing me.

"Beau is single," my cousin Luna whispers beside me. "Beau with his pants down would also be aesthetically pleasing."

I roll my eyes, blaming the overbearing photographer for now making me the center of the joke.

"Why don't you go for it then?" I tell her, turning the tables. Beau wasn't related to any of us besides Will, of course. "Cradle snatcher would suit you for once."

Luna pinches my arm softly. "Catty... what's wrong, cuz? You want to call dibs on him?"

"Uh... no," I mutter. "He's Will's brother. You don't break those rules."

She throws her back to laugh. "Edwards girls love breaking the rules."

It took the sun to slowly disappear for the photographer to call it a wrap. Thank fucking God. No chance in hell I would ever work a modeling career after experiencing that torture.

We are asked to take our seats at the table. Once again, I'm seated next to my single cousins because all the couples want to be next to their partners. I don't mind, given I'm away from my parents and can drink more.

Just like last night, the food comes out nonstop. I'm starving, or maybe knowing all this food is free makes it taste even better. My obsession with cheese is next level. I could eat plates of it and ignore the mains. The smellier, the tastier.

The sound of a fork tapping against the glass catches our attention as Eric raises a glass.

"On behalf of myself, the person who made this all happen, I'd like to raise a toast to the newlyweds. May this night be everything you've ever dreamed of."

Everyone raises their glasses, ignoring Eric's usual brag about his talents. Ava looks annoyed, and knowing her, she wants credit.

"I'd also like to raise a toast," Ava begins, dagger eyes straight at Eric. "It takes a village to make such magical events happen. I'm grateful to be part of the village."

"To raise a family," Eric corrects her.

"You didn't do everything," Ava bites back.

Luna is beside me, leaning back into her chair with a grin. "Oh, this is good wedding entertainment. Who do you think will reach out and pull the other's hair first?"

"Eric," my cousin Sienna answers. "For sure."

To avoid this escalating, Dad stands up and commands

attention. It's enough to make Eric and Ava stop. Just like always, everyone turns their attention to him because he has a way of owning a room full of people.

"These toasts never get easier, perhaps even harder as time goes on," he begins, then clears his throat. "Addison, it's not hard to find the right words to describe how much you mean to your mother and me. You've been a constant joy in our lives, always thinking about your family before yourself."

I can feel a tingle spread across my arm, like a match being lit inside my stomach with flames starting to soar. His tone feels directed at me, the whole constant joy and family before yourself.

"Your patience, kindness, and willingness to accept our guidance have made you the person you are today."

He's attacking me. I bow my head, willing to calm myself down as my hands tremble. How dare he use this moment to point out everything he hates about me.

"We are proud to call you our daughter, and now, we welcome you, Masen, as our son."

There are a lot of sighs, plus tears from Mom. *What's fucking new?*

As for me, he's done it again—made me feel like I'm the biggest disappointment in his life. I'll never live up to my sisters, so why bother?

I bow my head as speeches continue, allowing the noise to drown out. When the music starts again, I excuse myself to relieve the pressure inside my chest, ready to combust. The winery is spacious with plenty of room to sit by yourself and have a minute.

But my minute is interrupted.

"Are you okay?"

The familiar voice is behind me in the dark as I look out

at the rows of grapes in the distance—row after row, almost never-ending.

"Yes, no. I don't know," I mumble.

Beau sits down beside me on the stone step. The scent of his aftershave is very alluring, but I quickly ignore it because it's just another reminder of what's missing in my life. He pulls out a cigarette. Ugh... what a disgusting habit.

"You don't have to put this pressure on yourself." He puffs.

I shake my head. "What are you talking about?"

"The pressure to live up to your siblings. Thinking you're disappointing your parents."

"I... I don't know what you're talking about," I lie.

"Hey," he calls softly. "Look at me."

Slowly, I shift my eyes from the vineyard and stare into his eyes. Something unusual passes between us in a moment of silence, but I tell myself my emotions are all over the place. Nothing makes sense, but everything is crystal clear at the same time. Again, all over the place because that doesn't make sense.

"You, Alexa Edwards, are going to do great things. One day it will just fall into place."

"What will fall into place?"

"Life," he answers with his lips curving up into a warm smile, followed by a puff of smoke expelling from his mouth. "Whatever it is you're meant to do or meant to be, it will all just fall into place. Fuck everyone, just live life on your terms."

"How do you know? Are you living life on your terms?"

"I'm wise, a whole four months older than you." He chuckles, then knocks my shoulder gently with his. "C'mon, I've been around your dad long enough to know the real problem here. You're both equally as stubborn as each other."

"I am not stubborn," I almost yell, his eyes widening in surprise with a grin accompanying it. "That's not a nice thing to say to a woman."

He rubs his chin, looking oddly handsome at this moment. "Yeah, but I think of you like a sister, so it's fine to call you that."

And that's my cue to stop all these maddening thoughts.

A sister... of course. As I said, we were forced to play nice and taught the importance of family from a young age.

"I guess I better go back before they start calling me the black sheep of the family. Wait, maybe it's too late for that."

Beau reaches out to grab my wrist to stop me. My eyes fall to where his hand grips. At the same time, I fight back the sensations spreading across my entire body. The temperature around me elevates, making it hard to breathe. He's family... he thinks of me like a sister.

"You're never alone. Just remember that."

My eyes dart toward his, matching his deep stare. *Why is he looking at me this way? Like there's something he wants to say but can't.*

"I know," I say in a whisper as he releases the grip on my wrist.

"Good." He almost chokes on his response like he's struggling with his thoughts, but then he pulls himself out by taking another drag. "Until next time, Alexa."

I nod, then smile. "Yeah, next time. Maybe lay off the smoking if you wanna live, though."

A smirk spreads across his face before he extinguishes the cigarette on the ground. His eyes slowly drag to meet mine as he bites the corner of his lip.

"See, you break one bad habit and need another."

"Maybe you think you need something bad, but again, another habit to break."

The hazel orbs stare back at me, silent but heavy in a weighted gaze. "You know me, can't stay good for too long."

At least the bad boy knows his weakness.

Maybe it's not a weakness but his strength. Guards up, never get hurt.

"I'll get the bail money ready," I tease, unable to hide my grin. "I'm just a DM away."

Beau bows his head with a soft laugh. "I'll remember that, Miss Edwards."

EIGHT

As the sun rises in the morning, my body refuses to sleep in despite screaming at me to rest.

I'd barely slept, maybe three hours at most. The night ended only a few hours ago when Rocky started taking his clothes off after multiple rounds of shots. He got his hands on Cognac, an awful-tasting drink, but apparently, the French people enjoy it.

The newlyweds had long gone, saying goodbye to everyone before retiring to their own place for some alone time. The moment they left, the party turned into something else.

Beau disappeared early. I'm not sure where, nor did I ask. For all I know, he's Bruce Wayne pretending to be Batman to fight crime.

That, or he hooked up with someone in town.

People drank more, and the music got louder. To Eric's amusement, Rocky got fed up with his suit and began stripping off.

When we all caught a glimpse of the leopard print

underwear, I took the opportunity to excuse myself to bed. Some things can never be unseen.

Inside the kitchen, there are three personal chefs preparing breakfast. I offer them a smile, then ask politely for coffee since my brain is yet to wake up. Of all the guests, I'm the only one accustomed to the time zone, making it easier for me to be awake at this time, even though a little more sleep would have been nice. The irony of this, my father is nowhere to be seen—the one person who always wakes up each morning before anyone else.

I walk outside to the patio area, where a small wicker table and two chairs sit. The view is impressive—just open fields of the countryside and a lot of silence. I'm not used to it, having spent my time in the city for the last few months, but after a long day with all my family, I welcome the momentary silence.

"Morning," a voice behind me yawns.

Ava is wearing a burgundy robe with a coffee in hand. She takes a seat across from me, yawning again. Her hair is a mess, tied into a bun, yet she still looks beautiful even though she's makeup-free. Okay, maybe the dark circles make her look older, but I'll keep that observation to myself.

"Are you awake before your kids? How is that possible?"

"It's a miracle. Promise me you'll enjoy your life before you have kids," she says while taking a sip from the small espresso cup. "Sleep is the greatest gift to ever exist."

My eyes fall to the tabletop, but as quick as it does, I raise them again with a forced smile. "I like thinking about me for once."

"So, nothing from Cole?"

I shake my head. "I unfollowed him on socials."

"Good move, nothing worse than staying friends with an ex."

"You unfollowed all your ex-boyfriends?"

Ava nods. "Any guy I'd slept with."

"Wow." I chuckle, surprised at her admission. "That's a lot of unfollowing."

Across the table, Ava presses her lips flat in annoyance but then breaks out into a knowing smile. "Yeah, whatever... so I have a past."

"Too bad Austin can't unfollow his ex."

"Funny," she responds with sarcasm laced in her voice. "Lucky, I'm an understanding wife."

"I don't know how you do it," I admit, wondering how anyone stays near their ex-partner. "You, Millie, even Mom and Dad with Uncle Julian."

Ava lets out a sigh, relaxing her shoulders as she enjoys the view around us. It's hard to believe she's a mother of two daughters. Ava has always been the selfish one, thinking about herself. Look at her now, all responsibility and a changed woman.

"When you find that person, no one else matters. Ex-lovers are exes for a reason. It was never meant to be."

"True, although I don't know how Dad managed to move on and be around Uncle Julian."

A small laugh escapes Ava to the point she almost chokes on the hot coffee. I watch on, waiting to see what happens.

"Oh God," she rasps, clearing her throat. "Look, Dad is as alpha as you can get. The problem with him is if he was to lose his wife or sister, he wouldn't be able to survive. So, he has no choice. It sucks to be Lex Edwards, huh?"

"Oh, sure," I drag. "Totally sucks to be a controlling father too."

"C'mon, give him a break. You're high maintenance."

"Um, hello?" I almost yell, my eyes widening in disbelief from the irony. "You're high maintenance. Everyone knows that."

"I'm not high maintenance, perhaps dramatic at times."

"Dramatic would be an understatement." I snort.

"My point is, cut Dad some slack, okay? You are going against everything he says. It doesn't make life easier on any of us."

"Ava, I disagree with his rules. I'm an adult now, have been for a while."

Ava remains quiet, her piercing green eyes watching and making me uncomfortable. She's rarely quiet, so when she is, you can expect verbal diarrhea of thoughts at any moment.

"No matter how old we grow, we always need our dad. There's no shame in it. We will always be Daddy's little girls. Be grateful we are blessed to be given life with a man who will do anything to protect us."

"Easy for you to say. You're his favorite."

Ava shakes her head in disagreement. "Trust me. It's Millie."

"Millie? No way, she's too stubborn like Mom. Plus, the whole sneaking around with Will drama? Maybe, Addy, she's the goody-two-shoes."

We both laugh in unison, then let out a sigh seconds apart.

"I think you're right," Ava continues, trying to catch her breath. "But listen, and I'm serious here, be careful, okay?"

"I know," I tell her. "Come back in one piece."

"And you know my home is open... and my wallet. If you don't want to call Mom or Dad, whatever. Austin and I are here if you need us."

Despite my years of clashing with Ava, of all my sisters, she has never not come through for me. There's comfort in

her words, and for the first time in months, I feel more confident to continue with my travels without the fear of failing
at life.

"You just want a built-in babysitter," I joke.

"Yes!" She giggles, throwing her head back. "But I think
Millie will fight for you. Just remember, if it's down to us,
Austin is a heart surgeon, so that always comes in handy."

"Sure, I guess, if I need heart surgery," I joke, grinning.
"But Will is a billionaire. They can pay me good money."

"Are you forgetting Will is Lex Edwards junior? Do you
really want to be around that? And they're always having
sex everywhere. It'll be like living with Mom and Dad
again."

My stomach churns at the thought. "Gross, why would
you say that? Anyways, it's not like you're celibate.
Everyone knows you fucked Austin in the pool house last
year at the Fourth of July party."

"That was Will and Millie!"

"Really? Addy and Luna swore it was you."

Ava's eyes light up. "Oh, so speaking of Luna, guess
who I saw hot and heavy against the wall last night."

"Who?"

"Luna and Cruz."

The news surprises me. I didn't see that coming at all.
Luna never mentioned Cruz, but I'm going to assume they
both got drunk and needy.

"Do you think he did it to get over Addy?" I ask.

"Nah, I think he's genuinely happy for Masen and
Addy," she admits. "But I think Luna was drunk and
wanted to get laid. I'm surprised, given she does older men,
but Cruz is hot, plus he has the whole footballer thing going
for him. Luna is probably on an ego high right now. Women
want Cruz, and she got him into bed."

"You think they actually slept together?"

Ava sneers. "C'mon, Alexa. Don't be naïve. This isn't high school anymore. The way I saw them, they were one step away from it. Anyway, both of them disappeared after that. You do the math."

Luna is notorious for being open about her sex life. Personally, I didn't understand the whole instant attraction and taking it to the bedroom. However, it's not instant since they've known each other for years.

Either way, it's none of my business. I'm sure Ava would beg to differ.

"So, one last hurrah before you leave?"

My brows narrow the more her face lights up. "What does your hurrah entail?"

"Lunch, just us girls."

"And Eric?"

Ava throws her head back in amusement. "I think Eric is unable to join us."

"Hangover?"

"Let's just say if his Airbnb hosts weren't swingers, they probably are now."

"Oh God." I moan. "What is wrong with our family?"

"Where do I begin," Ava answers while laughing. "I'm sure we'll get all the answers at lunch. Once Eric wakes up and spills the beans in our group chat."

My shoulders move up and down, unable to hold back my laughter. I'm going to miss my family, but of everyone, I think I'm going to miss Ava the most.

Not that I would *ever* admit it to her face.

Some things are best left unsaid.

NINE

The best part about traveling through Europe is the freedom to be me without the pressure of my family's name.

No one knew who I was, or maybe if they did, they didn't care.

The anonymity relieved me of the expectations I've lived with my whole life. Our family wasn't celebrities by all means. It wasn't like the paparazzi followed us everywhere, but they still managed to keep an eye on what we did. They were strategic and targeted mostly my father at big events, not so much everyday life. In recent years, they slowed down because, frankly, my father is boring as fuck. He never did anything exciting to cause a media frenzy unless it was a colleague or associate embroiled in some scandal.

Ava became a target for a while, but it was only because she made sure her life was documented on social media for the purpose of content, as she likes to put it. Since becoming a mother, she's been careful to keep her daughters away from the limelight. I think it has a lot to do with

Austin not wanting his daughters exposed to the creeps of the world.

I said goodbye to my family over six months ago, two days after Masen and Addy said 'I do.' Mom struggled to say goodbye again, unable to compose herself when we hugged for the last time. She worried about me and even tried to slip some money into my purse. Her intentions came from a motherly place, but I was determined to make it on my own. That hadn't changed just because I spent a few days with them.

My sisters were dramatic with their goodbyes, ugly crying, of course. At the time, I was really not surprised if one of them, if not both, were knocked up. It would explain the hormonal mess they were that morning. So far, no announcements so my assumptions were wrong. They were just hot messes.

As for my father, the cold goodbye was enough for me to turn around and not look back. He embraced me, though it was stiff and not loving in any sort of way. It didn't upset me. I expect nothing more from him.

It was time to move on to my next adventure, where the best thing happened to me—April West.

April is nothing like me—unstoppable in her quest to live life to the fullest. We met in Ibiza when we realized the guy we were flirting with was trying to get us all into bed together. Now, I'm not one for threesomes, and the guy was so full of himself that we just had to teach him a lesson.

The lesson was telling him to book the expensive suite, but we never showed up. Instead, we spent the night drinking and laughing so hard I'll admit a tiny bit of pee came out during the barrels of laughter.

"Do you think the yellow bikini or polka dots?"

April is holding the hangers up, waiting for my opinion

as we stand in a small boutique store in Mykonos. Our lives have revolved around the pools and beaches, which warranted new swimwear. Also, we got a nice tip from an American businesswoman last night who felt sorry for us since it was a busy night and the crowd was rougher than usual.

"Yellow," I state firmly. "Polka dots are never a good idea."

"Wait... should I entertain a one-piece?"

A laugh expels so quickly, causing me to choke. When I finally catch my breath, I shake my head. "You, a one-piece? I don't think so."

"You're right. What would I do without you?"

"Be wearing a one-piece and never get laid," I joke.

"Speaking of getting laid, what happened last night with that tall, dark-haired beauty? Adrian, was it?"

I shrug, continuing to sort through the rack of swim-suits. "Not much, you know, we fooled around, but I wasn't into it."

Adrian was hot, sure. Halfway into it when he pulled a condom out, something didn't feel right. Panic overcame me, and I politely told him I had to go. He didn't look hurt, maybe frustrated. I shouldn't have put myself in the posi-tion to begin with when I had no intention of sleeping with him.

April places her hands on my shoulders. Her stare is fixated on mine with concern.

"I think you're broken. No man has made you feel that thrill since we've been together. I mean, Alexa, the men are throwing themselves at you, and you are stunning, my girl. I mean, how many times have you been approached by photographers to model? That's how beautiful you are. What the hell is happening?"

"I'm not broken," I answer defensively. "I'm just clearly not a one-night stand kind of gal. It just feels so rushed and zero connection."

"As long as you masturbate and still get off somehow."

"I'm not a robot." I chuckle. "I'm pretty self-sufficient when I need to be."

"Good," April says, removing her hands from my shoulders. "Okay, so let's talk about our plans for the next month before I lose you forever to some sorority."

April's words sink deep, causing a heaviness to form inside my chest. My shoulders slump, the reality of my father's demands drawing closer as time passes. Time is of the essence. Only three weeks left before I'm back under his rules and applying for colleges as originally agreed upon.

It already started, the subtle emails checking in on how I'm doing. At first, I fell for it and answered as if I was talking to a long-lost friend. Then, he followed with links to university programs.

For the most part, I did my best not to dwell on the future. Since I was nineteen already, having celebrated my birthday while traveling, it wasn't impossible to get into college, and my father made sure I knew that.

"Can we not go there?" I mumble, finding myself in a funk. "You're killing my buzz."

"Buzz?" April chuckles. "You've been in a mood all day. Periods?"

"We're period sisters, remember? I had mine last week with you. We bought that whole tub of ice cream and watched *The Notebook*. We cried, then spent the night on the toilet with cramps."

April scrunches her nose. "Never again."

Our three weeks together flew by like it was minutes. The closer we got, the more I drank, expecting it all to go away like some miracle. I almost expected my father to call me on the day of the one year spent abroad, but he didn't. Instead, a month passed, and nothing from him.

Mom continued to check in on me, but she mentioned nothing about me returning. It was like something out of the twilight zone, and cocky me thought I got away with it.

That was until I got an email from my father with an attachment. It was the plane ticket home. I must board his private plane from Heathrow to Los Angeles in exactly one week.

"It's not that bad," April says softly while sitting beside me as I stare at my suitcase blankly. "We'll go back together."

I shake my head. "I can't ask you to go back."

"What else am I going to do? Just like you, I traveled to do something greater. Turns out not as fun if you don't have someone to enjoy it with."

April's family lives in Los Angeles too. She only moved there a year ago from Arizona when her mother remarried. Her mother married some rich guy five years younger than her. According to April, she married for the money since April's mom had her at fifteen and struggled their whole lives financially.

Of the times we spoke about her family, she didn't hate her stepfather. April said she chose to keep to herself and allow her mom to live her new life. Her stepfather was young, only thirty, so it makes the dynamics awkward. I kind of feel sorry for her, completely understanding why she chose to travel after graduation rather than stick around to watch her mom and new daddy play husband and wife.

"April—" The phone beside me beeps with a text message from my sister, Ava. My eyes quickly read the message.

AVA

I thought it's best this came from me, and
you didn't stumble on it during scrolling.

There's a screenshot that appears next. My eyes zoom in to get a better look. It's Cole with his arms around Madaline. I remember her from English class. She wasn't a mean girl or anything. She was nice, chilled, and caused no trouble.

It's the arms around her that my eyes fixate on. It's the protruding belly. The room temperature rises, making me anxious and uncomfortable. My vision blurs, but I widen my eyes to focus so I can read the post's caption.

We are finally ready to announce our baby girl is due just before Christmas. I never expected to love someone so deeply, but I can't wait to meet you soon.

The bile rises in my throat. My head shakes from the sheer shock. I cover my mouth, rushing to the toilet before I empty my stomach into the toilet bowl with a loud cry. April rushes up behind me, rubbing my back while pulling my hair from my face.

My sobs become louder, the hurt rippling through me like a hurricane destined to destroy everything in its sight. The walls of my chest tighten, making breathing hard, and my breaths come out like chokes.

"What have I done?" I cry, unable to control the pain consuming my whole heart. *"It could have been us."*

"Alexa, what happened?"

The words refuse to come out, the pain crippling me to the point of despair. How was I to know he would want this? The Cole I knew only wanted to pursue his football career. Not once did he give me any inkling of a future with children. If anything, he didn't want anything standing in the way of him chasing his dreams. Football... all he wanted was football.

"I can't go back," I sob, shaking my head repeatedly. "I can't go back and face him."

"Who, Alexa?"

"Cole, my ex. I can't go back home and face him. I don't know what I'll do if I see him."

April doesn't say anything else. Being the good friend she is, her silence is exactly what I need. My guilt is making enough noise. Screaming and forcing me to relive the nightmare I'd been trying to escape the last year while traveling.

"Alexa, right now, you don't have to do anything," April eventually says softly. "But going back home is inevitable."

"I won't go back and live under my father's rules. He's the reason this all happened," I sputter angrily.

"Okay, okay." April attempts to soothe my anger. "My door is always open. I say we go back to LA, and you stay with me. There's plenty of room. Mom is always out spending Hunter's money."

"Hunter?" I ask through thin, strained sobs.

"Yeah, stepdaddy. I call him Hunter since that's his name, and it would be awkward to call him Daddy since he's like ten years older than me."

The corners of my lips slowly move up, but they fall right back down as quickly as they do.

"They won't mind me staying?"

"The house is like eleven thousand square feet. Too big for three people, trust me, we never see each other, and it's like a ghost town. There's guest quarters, and they won't mind. As I said, they're never home and wouldn't even know you're there."

It's not like I have a choice. There is no other option for me.

Going back home to live with my father would remind me of the mistakes I've made. As for attending college, why should I reward him for ruining my life?

The decision is made. I'll go back to the States but under my own terms. April's offering her home which I'll stay in until I get a job and can take care of myself.

It can't be that hard, I tell myself as I take a deep breath trying to control my emotions and get a grip on reality.

I'm Alexa Edwards. If there's anything good my father has passed down to me, it's my determination to succeed.

And I'll do it exactly how I want to do it.

Without his help.

TEN

April was not exaggerating when she said her house was a ghost town and the chances of running into someone would be slim.

It's been exactly one week since we got on the plane back to Los Angeles. It wasn't my father's private plane. Instead, it was a plane ticket flying economy next to a man who snored so loud when he slept and a woman who kept complaining about everything. The number of times she called the air hostess was a joke. I didn't think it was possible to be embarrassed by a stranger's behavior, but this time I was. Some people should *never* leave their homes.

The worst part of all of this is I used my savings to buy this ticket. I didn't want a single cent from my father.

Of course, going against him caused drama in my family. My sisters were relentless in verbally abusing me over text messages. Well, Millie and Ava were. Addy was oddly quiet. I figured she was too busy being a newlywed to get involved.

Mom was pissed. Her tone was cold when I explained to her my reasons, all of which came out as one big fat lie which made no sense. In the end, I gave up trying and basically said they had to deal with my decision.

At the time, I felt somewhat empowered standing on my own two feet and making decisions without thinking about anything else. Then, I slowly began to realize that without a college degree or further studies, no one wanted to touch me. In Europe, hospitality roles were everywhere, and no one cared what I had or hadn't done. Living in the States is a completely different story.

"Look, you've gone on four interviews this week and haven't heard a thing," April reminds me as we sit in the den, trying to find something to watch. "Will you please take me up on my offer?"

My confidence is shattered because two of those jobs already emailed to say I wasn't successful, and chances are the other two will follow. They weren't even anything special. Just junior office jobs involving answering the phone and filing.

"You've already done so much, like letting me stay here."

"And?" April raises her voice. "You need money, right? Why not take the job?"

"Well, firstly, there's no guarantee I have the job. You're assuming your stepfather will hire me based on being your friend. If you say he's some rich CEO like my father, chances are he doesn't give a shit who the person is. If they don't have the skills or education, they don't have it."

April lets out a frustrated sigh. "When are you going to just trust the universe?"

Laughter comes out of my mouth, followed by an unflattering snort. When I manage to calm down, reality shines its wavy red flags to remind me of the cold hard truth.

"The universe is not my bestie. I don't believe in the

whole universe thing," I drag with a sarcastic tone. "You sound just like my sister, Ava."

"Okay, so forget the universe for a second. So what if you've had rejections? It builds character. Supposed to make you stronger, or something like that."

"Yeah, well, unfortunately, it doesn't build my bank account."

"I can lend you money," April offers.

April isn't wealthy by any means, but she is savvy in saving what she does have. Her car is some old Jeep gifted to her by her uncle. It blows out smoke and has rust around the edges, yet she loves it like it's a brand-new Lamborghini or something.

During our travels, she flirted with guys to get free dinners and drinks, saving every dollar for no apparent reason. She's on the fence about going to college but is considering studying abroad just to get out of LA.

"No, you've done so much already." I glance at the time on my phone. My shoulders tense when I see it's almost time to leave for dinner at my parents' house. "I'm going to shower and get changed. You sure you don't want to come to dinner?"

"Why, you sound nervous?"

"I just don't want to go alone. If you come, my father won't raise his voice and remind me of how much of a disappointment I am to the family."

The moment it leaves my mouth, my phone pings with a text message.

AVA

Thank me later. I'm joining you for dinner tonight. Someone needs to keep a tally as you and Dad battle it out.

"Argh, never mind. Apparently, Ava is joining us."

"See, the universe made sure it all worked out," April gloats with a grin.

I yank the velvet cushion from beside me and throw it at her head. "Enough with the universe talk, weirdo."

Upon entering the house, the smell of something delicious lingers in the air. If I'm not mistaken, it's Mom's homemade lasagna and garlic bread. When it comes to cooking, her food is always amazing.

The smell is not the only thing I notice—it's how everything is in the same position, and nothing has changed. Without even thinking, a sigh escapes me while I take it all in. This place still feels like home, despite my moving out, and so many memories fight for attention the more I observe my surroundings.

Mom walks out of the kitchen and notices me. Our last conversation was strained, but she manages a smile to welcome me.

"Come join me in the kitchen." She motions for me to follow, which I do. Inside the kitchen, the burner is on and boiling something. The aroma is even stronger, but all I can think about is the fact that it's been months since I saw her, nearly a year, and she hasn't offered to embrace me.

I reach my arms out and move close to her, wrapping my arms around her like a little girl. Inside my embrace, I feel her relax, then let out a breath before she kisses me on the forehead and caresses my cheek with the back of her hand.

"Alexa," she whispers. "You've grown so much."

"And you've not aged one bit."

Mom laughs. "Eric thinks I should take the plunge and do Botox. He took a photo of my face and drew lines where he thought I needed it. Then, Kate got annoyed and took an all-body shot of him and pointed out where he needed lipo."

"Lipo? Eric? His body is toned to perfection."

"It is, but she just wanted to make him paranoid and prove a point."

"And?"

Mom cringes. "It didn't end well. Eric cried and said he thought he had a thigh problem and had been in denial for years. It was so dramatic that we spent the rest of the day convincing him he had absolutely no thigh problem. It was a joke, or perhaps a lesson, which backfired."

"Poor you and Kate."

"So, I let him book in my Botox because I felt sorry for him."

"Mom," I shout with a grin. "You don't need it."

"I know, so when the appointment comes round, Adriana said she'll go."

"Thank God," I say with relief. "Although, Aunt Adriana doesn't need it either."

Mom opens the oven and pulls out the lasagna, as I suspected. The cheese on the top is bubbling to perfection, making my stomach grumble from how mouthwatering it looks.

As she places it down on the countertop, she removes her oven mitts and then focuses back on me.

"Your father is not here," she begins with, then continues. "So, I'm going to ask between us girls, how you are?"

I force a smile, then realize Mom's not the one I'm angry at even though our last conversation didn't end well. "I'm trying to adjust. It's fun staying with April."

"And what about money?"

"Mom," I say, lowering my voice. "I'll make do."

"Alexa, I'm a mother. My job is to worry about my kids even though they may not be kids anymore."

My head shakes in disagreement. "You shouldn't worry, Mom. Be proud that you raised women who can make it on their own."

Mom stills her movements, but her eyes continue to watch me. "I'm here to talk about anything."

"I know Mo—" The engine of my father's car interrupts as it pulls into the driveway and parks out back. I bow my head, close my eyes, and take a deep breath. *It's just dinner... two hours at best. I can do this.*

The back door opens, and Dad walks in dressed in his usual suit. His eyes instantly gaze upon me, but he's quick to distract himself by placing his keys and phone down on the counter before he kisses Mom hello.

"Alexa, it's nice for you to join us."

"Thank you, Dad."

The conversation comes to a crashing halt until Dad excuses himself to freshen up before dinner. Before Mom can get a word in, another car pulls up. The loud music blaring a trending song is enough for me to know it's Ava.

Minutes later, Ava walks in looking extra nice in a maxi dress which she paired with matching wedges. Her hair is French braided, something I'm jealous of since Ava can braid her own hair, but I never could, no matter how much I tried.

"Alexa," Ava squeals, then fans herself as if she didn't see me on the weekend. "It's been forever."

"Ha-ha," I mock, then grab the plates Mom has put out. "Maybe help me set the table?"

"Sure."

Inside the dining room, when I'm standing alone with Ava, I quickly grab her arm before my parents walk in.

"We need a game plan," I whisper.

"For what?"

"Getting me out of here."

Ava folds her arms, tilting her head. "Why?"

"Quit playing dumb. Dad is going to crucify me for not going to college."

"And?"

This time, my arms fold in frustration. "What do you mean and? The whole purpose of you being here was to defend me."

"I never said I was going to defend you," she corrects me. "I said I was going to watch... with popcorn."

A loud groan escapes me at the same time my parents walk in. The mood in the room instantly shifts, forcing Mom to encourage us to take a seat and begin eating.

Ava carries most of the conversation, thank God. She's been blessed with the gift of talking nonstop, no matter what topic you throw at her.

"Anyway..." she finally takes a breath, "... that's what's been happening with the online store. Hopefully, this new marketing campaign will give it the facelift I envision for my brand."

Mom smiles politely, then shifts her gaze to me.

"It's really nice to have you join us."

"Thanks, Mom." I smile in return. "The food is delicious as always. It's been a while since I've eaten something so tasty."

"I thought April's place had chefs or something?" Ava questions.

"She does, but it doesn't seem right for them to cook for

me..." I admit, then rush, "... you know, because I'm a guest for now."

A cold breeze sweeps across my skin, but no windows or doors are open as I look around. It dawns on me the cool air is not so much the air but the tension between my father and me. The cold snap, cold front, or whatever you want to call it, is because his opinion of my behavior will have to come out tonight. There's no chance he will keep it to himself. Not Lex Edwards, he always has to have the last word.

"And how do you expect to support yourself, Alexandra?" he questions in a condescending tone. "Stay with your friend until what exactly?"

Boom.

My eyes fall to the napkin sitting on my lap. The plain white fabric is like a blank canvas where I can paint my thoughts and emotions, blocking out his noise since he chooses to project all his bullshit onto me.

"Dad," Ava begins with, trying her best to mediate between us. "We were all young—"

"Ava, this is not your battle."

His cold stance on my sister is enough for me to raise my eyes to meet his.

"You're right," I state firmly, watching as his head draws back. He quickly realizes he's shown emotion, then snaps into a stern glance once again. "This is not Ava's battle. It's also not my battle. It's your battle. You can't control me anymore, and it's eating you alive."

"Alexa," Mom warns. "Your tone."

My lips purse, followed by a frown. "My tone? Look at your husband and reprimand him, not me."

I stand up, throwing my napkin on the table before Ava reaches out and touches my arm softly.

"Alexa, sit down," she says softly. "It'll be okay."

My head shakes involuntarily. "I refuse to sit at this table and be told how I'm going to fail in life without sticking to his rules."

"Alexandra!" My father's raised voice echoes in the dining room, startling all three of us. He slams his fist on the table, causing the silverware to rattle. "Why must you defy everything I say? What have I done to make you hate me this much, huh?"

If I look away, he will win. He will know his power over me still reigns. If I come back here, everything I've experienced in the last year will be wasted, like I'd escaped the dungeon, but the four walls will trap me once again for as long as I need his help.

"I'm leaving," I mutter.

"C'mon, Alexa," Ava begs.

For a brief moment, I glance at Mom, staring absently at her hands. Despite my father practically bursting at the seams filled with anger, her still pose and blank stare speaks much louder words.

I've let her down, and quite possibly, that's what is hurting the most right now.

My hands reach into my pocket as I retrieve my car and house keys. With a deep breath, I place them down on the table.

"I won't be needing these. They belong to you."

I don't look at my father nor allow him to say another word. Instead, I walk away toward the front door with a greater weight on my shoulders. Everything I need or want, I've let go of.

It's now just me fighting to survive.

The door closes behind me but opens in a rush as Ava runs out, all huffed. Her eyes are red, and her lips quiver.

She crosses her arms when I stop but lowers her gaze so I can't see them.

"Why, Alexa? What happened to you? You're so angry at them, and none of this makes sense."

The quiver in her voice and her emotions surfacing triggers something inside me. My stomach churns, and even though we're standing outside, the heat against my skin has a chokehold on me like I can't even breathe.

"Ava, don't—"

She rushes toward me, pulling me against her and holding me tight. In the arms of my big sister, the walls inside of me begin to crumble. A tear escapes me as I shake my head, willing it to stop.

"I'm here, Alexa. I'm here with no judgment," she offers.

"I know," I whisper. "But I can't, not now. I'm not ready."

And for the first time in my life, I admitted the pain I carried was never going to go away. It followed me wherever I went, and time did not erase it either.

"When you're ready..." she trails off.

I pull away slowly. "I know you're here, Ava. But I need to prove to myself that I can do this alone... without Dad's help."

"But why, Alexa? What's so bad about having Dad's support?"

"Please, just let me do what I need to do."

Ava lets me go but keeps close. Without a car, I'd have to call an Uber or ask Ava. As I look down at my phone, I realize my phone and bill are linked to my father. A long-winded sigh escapes me. Why is seeking independence so hard?

Or perhaps, why the fuck am I so stubborn?

"I'm assuming you need a ride home?"

I nod, allowing my pride to take a back seat for a moment. Some of these are worth arguing with and others not so much.

"What are the chances of a magic carpet pulling up at any moment?" I manage a small smile and then sigh. "Thank you."

"At least I can check out the new digs you're staying at."

"Actually, I kind of need a favor. Do you have a nice pantsuit or outfit I can borrow for an interview?"

Ava laughs softly as we both enter her car. "Are we impressing a hot CEO or some old dude we don't want anywhere near our panties?"

I shudder at the thought. "Gross, I would never. It reminds me of the time Eric told me one of his clients had a fetish for used panties. The more they were used, the more money they were worth."

"It's true. There's a market for it. The crustier, the better."

"Okay," I moan while cringing. "You took it way too far. How about a nice outfit that makes me look mature and not like some angsty college dropout?"

"You must attempt college to be a dropout," Ava teases, lightening the somber mood that clouded tonight. "I'm good with my outfits, but I don't know if I'm that good."

"You're the queen of fashion. You'll come up with something," I tell her while grinning.

"Challenge accepted."

ELEVEN

My pants are too tight and bunch up between my legs, making sitting very uncomfortable.

Ava insisted I wear pants instead of wearing a skirt to impress. If I want to be taken seriously, showing my legs is not the way. Also, something about pantsuits is so in right now. Regardless, I send her a quick text to vent my frustrations.

ME

> Your pants are giving me camel toe. This is worse than showing a leg.

The bubble appears at record speed, much like her response.

AVA

> I'm with Eric. He says to be careful. There's good camel toe, and there's bad camel toe.

I abandon the conversation because, in my opinion, there's no such thing as good camel-toe. Besides, I need to focus on this interview and forget about these stupid pants.

As much as it pained me to do so, I took April up on her offer to accept an interview for a job at her stepfather's company. It would have been nice to have at least met him, given I'm staying at his place, but he hasn't been home since. Apparently, he travels a lot which is why April said the house is always empty.

I met April's mother, Kathy, who is nice enough if you ignore the whole being hung-up-on-money thing. She spent most of her time shopping or vacationing with her new circle of rich friends. According to April, she was never like that, and for the most part, had a decent childhood raised by Kathy despite them scrapping for money.

Money changes everyone.

The once-doting mother no longer cares what her daughter does. I know April is hurt by the change but refuses to dwell on it. She's a glass-half-full kind of girl and is always trying to focus on the positives.

Yeah, the universe and all that bullshit.

Inside the very modern lobby, I glance around and notice I'm not the only girl sitting there. There are five of us, and all of the others appear to be the same age as me. Of course, they're all wearing short dresses. Here I am dressed like some mom with pants riding so far up my vagina.

The pantsuit is navy and simple in its cut. Ava suggested a classic white blouse beneath and even allowed me to borrow her tan Louboutins. Thank God we're the same size in everything because it pays off at times like this, except for the whole camel-toe part. Maybe Ava's vagina is smaller than mine.

My hair is pinned back into a tight bun which keeps it out of my face and professional. As I try not to focus on my nerves, an older woman comes out of the elevator and calls for an Ella. The blonde girl sitting across from me stands up, almost tripping on her heels, then follows the lady.

This happens again with Selina, Harriet, and Emily, all their names I'd learned while I waited for one hour until it was my turn.

"Alexandra," the older lady finally calls my name.

With a smile, I stand up and follow her into the elevator. I'm unsure what to say or if the protocol is to keep quiet. As a kid, my dad often reminded me of the importance of introducing myself so that everyone knows my name. Some things stick, I guess.

Quickly, I extend my hand. "I'm Alexandra Edwards. It's nice to meet you."

The lady looks confused, then nods. "Meredith Hancock. I'm Mr. Cash's Executive Assistant."

"It's nice to meet you, Mrs. Hancock."

"Meredith, please. Leave the formalities to Mr. Cash."

"Of course," I say with a smile.

April gave me no information or inkling as to what today entailed. I knew there was no way they would just hire me despite her saying she got me the job. All of a sudden, the nerves come back, but this time, even more so than before. I find myself fidgeting, though I quickly force myself to stop.

The elevator door opens to level four. As Meredith exits, I follow her to a small room where there is a computer. There is nothing in the room but three walls and a window that looks toward another building.

"Take a seat," Meredith instructs, gesturing to the chair. "You'll have thirty minutes to complete an online exam which will test your ability to perform in certain situations. It's followed by a typing test. You will be tested for speed and accuracy."

Typing test? My heart races. I'm no professional typist unless responding to a text from Ava because she's about to order a hideous outfit, which you'll know she'll regret later, then blame it on me for not talking her out of it.

Meredith leaves the room with minimal instructions. She only added to press any key, and the exam will begin. Although she didn't call it an exam, it feels exactly like I'm back in high school, making this extremely unsettling.

Taking a deep breath, I sit down on the office chair. I press the letter K on the keyboard for the screen to illuminate. The questionnaire appears, and given I only have thirty minutes to complete all of this, I straighten my shoulders while giving myself a pep talk. Then, I dive straight into the questions.

There are only ten questions and scenarios of what I would do in particular situations. I do my best to answer them, trying to think of what I should do versus what I would want to do. I mean, let's be honest, the question about your boss running late and not being able to pick up his dry cleaning has me rolling my eyes. I'm praying this role doesn't involve any errands like this, but then again, it's not like I have a choice right now.

Money is money. I need it or apologize to my father and ask him to take me back.

My stupid thoughts keep distracting me before I glance at the time in the corner of the screen. I only have ten minutes left. *Shit.*

Panicking, I move on to the next question, but instead, it's the section testing my typing speed and accuracy. There's a paragraph on the screen which I'm supposed to copy as quickly as possible. The timer begins, and I type as fast as I can, trying not to make any errors. Before I know it, my time is up, and the door opens with Meredith standing behind me.

"Thank you, Miss Edwards, for your time today," Meredith announces in a formal tone.

"Is that it?" I blurt out, then quickly try to redeem myself. "I apologize. I meant to say, is there any formal interview or perhaps meeting Mr. Cash?"

Meredith is writing in her notebook, eyes down, barely acknowledging me. If I have to say her age, she'd be much older than Mom, maybe pushing mid-sixties. Not that it matters, but it's clear she has no time for young women like me.

"The role primarily reports to me," she states firmly. "All I'm interested in is how quick, efficient, and responsive you are in certain situations."

Judging by her tone, it's obvious I didn't make an impression. There's no opportunity to even talk, given no interview or time to show what I can do.

My chest tightens as my stomach turns queasy. It's safe to say I didn't get the role, and I need to start focusing on Plan B. Not that there is a Plan B because April made it seem like her plan would solve all my problems. She's not to blame. If this is anyone's fault, it's clearly mine since I'm not good enough for anyone to hire.

I force a smile, deflated, but try to keep my shoulders poised as I walk out of the office and toward the elevator. There was no time to cry, given people occupied the elevator, and it would make me look like an emotional trainwreck.

I'm standing next to a pregnant woman who is breathing heavily. Oh God, what if we get stuck, and she gives birth in this elevator? My mind is a mess, so I focus on anything else which doesn't send my anxiety into a spiral of no return.

In the back corner, there is a man on his phone. He appears well-presented in a gray suit with a vest beneath the jacket. My eyes slowly trace down his waist until I reach his shoes. Huh, large. Eric's voice replays in my head, *"You can judge a man purely on his shoe size."*

I beg to differ. It must be some myth, not that I have much to compare to.

Slowly, my eyes drift past his crotch, which, okay—there is a trace of something. Shaking my head, I move up toward his face until I see him looking directly at me. Oh, shit! He doesn't look phased or bothered, keeping a straight expression but refusing to break eye contact.

I divert my eyes straight-ahead, trying to remember what he looked like seconds ago. He has a strong jawline with a freshly shaven face. I didn't quite catch the eye color, but they are dark, maybe brown.

My heart is beating faster than usual, but by the time I begin to panic again, the door opens, and everyone moves at a fast pace. I don't stop to think anymore, rushing outside and away from this hell of a place.

Out on the street, the usual California sun is trying its best to break through the heavy smog. Without a car, I'm again trying to figure out how to get around. April dropped me off, but she was meeting her aunt for lunch at some restaurant, so I need to find my way home.

Standing at the bus stop, I wait with an older woman and what appears to be her grandchild. It dawns on me that aside from field trips, I've never taken a bus in LA.

It takes fifteen minutes for the bus to arrive and open its doors. I follow the lady and what she does, paying for a ticket and taking a seat. There's an empty row toward the back of the bus, which I gladly take.

The drive is bumpy and long, giving me a lot of time to just stare out the window. I grow bored easily, then quickly check my phone. There are no texts or new emails. I follow with hopping onto my Insta and see a DM in the corner. Quickly tapping on the icon, most of it is stuff my sisters sent me, but then I see a message from an unknown username. It takes me a few minutes to figure out it must be Beau given the handle is Bromano. If I'm not mistaken, it's supposed to be like Bromance since the profile picture is some guy, maybe his bestie, posing with him.

BROMANO

My new professor's name is Alex Edwards. Thought you'd like to know how awkward economics is for me now. At least she's fun to look at.

I shake my head with a grin, but just as I'm about to respond, things start to look familiar. We're on the same street as my high school. The nostalgia is overwhelming. So many times, I'd driven down this street with Cole's hand resting on my knee as we talked about all the things we were going to do once we graduated.

Now, I'm here without a job or even a permanent place to stay while he's playing happy families.

The reality is brutal with its force, but I refuse to break down on a bus in front of a bunch of strangers. Just like inside the elevator, I try to think of anything else to distract me.

This is too hard. Maybe I should just go back.

My phone vibrates in my hand, interrupting my depressive thoughts. I quickly hit answer, not recognizing the number but pick it up in case it's a job I've applied for.

"Hello?"

"Am I speaking with Alexandra Edwards?"

"Yes." I clear my throat and sit up to pay attention. "I'm Alexandra."

"It's Meredith Hancock. Have I caught you at an inconvenient time?"

"Not at all," I lie.

"Good. I'd like to offer you the role of junior assistant."

My eyes widen as my breath catches in my throat. I open my mouth to talk, but words don't come out. With a quick swallow, I try again, careful not to stammer.

"You'd like to offer me the role?"

"Yes," Meredith confirms. "I can email across all the details and employment forms if you'd like to accept."

"Of course, I accept," I answer in disbelief, with a smile breaking loose. "I mean to say thank you. This means so much to me."

"Good," she responds, then continues. "Congratulations, Alexandra. I'll be in touch once you respond to the email."

TWELVE

The universe is finally on my side.

Damn, April has finally gotten to me.

This could be the start of a new life, one I've dreamed of for such a long time. I quickly press on my phone again, dialing Ava's number. The phone rings for the longest time as I tap my foot impatiently on the dirty floor. I'm going to have to catch the bus every single goddamn day until I can save some money to buy my own car.

I guess it could be so much worse.

"Hey, what's up?" Ava answers quickly. "I'm kind of in the middle of something."

"Kind of in the middle of what?" I ask, cringing.

"God, nothing like that," she claims. "Besides, it's like midday, and I've got one kid who refuses to take a nap and another who is completely zonked out on the couch. Do you know what that means?"

"What does that mean?"

"It means their naptimes are no longer synced. I have to somehow figure out how to get things done because I've lost two hours of freedom."

"Just call Mom to help you."

"I can't just run to Mom every time I need help," Ava raises her voice, but it wakes whoever is asleep, so she lowers her tone to barely above a whisper.

"Why? She loves your kids and babysitting," I remind her. "She says it all the time."

"Maybe because Mom still has a career. She runs her own business and manages people. Mom's still girl-bossing at her age. Dumping my kids on her is unfair because I'm having a bad day."

I'm all out of ideas on how to help Ava, growing bored with her dilemma.

"Okay, so what about Millie? Dump them on her."

"Why are you calling?" she responds impatiently. "It's not about my kids."

"Right, okay. So, I wanted to tell you I got the job."

A crackling sound over the speaker sounds like Ava dropped the phone.

"Oh my god. We've been talking about my situation, which you don't care about anyway, and all this time, you could've told me you got the job. Congrats, sis," she rushes in excitement. "Give me all the details but wait a minute, let me get comfortable because River looks like she is just about to pass out. Maybe my talking to you is helping, so I probably shouldn't stop talking."

I glance at the window to see I'm not so far from Ava's place.

"I'm on the bus, about to hop off," I tell her while standing up. "I was hoping I could come over because I need a new wardrobe."

"Fine, see you soon."

"When I agreed to lend you one outfit for the interview, I didn't agree to lend you an entire wardrobe for your new corporate career," Ava complains as I sift through her wardrobe and pick out items to wear.

Hanging over my arm is a nice gray pencil skirt, a black buttoned shirt, and a matching blazer to the skirt.

"But you're so pretty and talented," I coerce in my sweetest tone. "You're the best big sister ever."

Ava's girls managed to fall asleep simultaneously, which is why she's hovering over me and watching what I take. When I reach to pull out a nice beige dress, she instantly slaps my hand and demands I put it back. Something about Valentino and vintage.

The baby monitor she's carrying in her hand makes a crackling sound before a cry blares through the speaker. Ava's shoulders fall, followed by a heavy sigh.

"Freedom is over. I'll meet you downstairs when you're done."

I spend another twenty minutes going through her clothes since she has a lot. Of all my sisters, Ava's wardrobe is like the women's department at Macy's. Racks and racks of clothing, all of which are organized into colors and or styles.

When I'm finished, I borrow two pairs of pants, three skirts, and four blouses. It's enough for me to mix and match until I can afford to buy my own clothes.

Ava is inside the kitchen with River, sitting in her highchair, attempting to eat some fruit. River has grown so much in the last year. Walking, somewhat talking, she's a mini-Austin and it's super cute. It's not just her, everyone has grown. I'm only two months away from turning the big twenty. Time sure did fly when I was having fun in Europe.

Austin arrives home from some meeting to pick up

Emmy. She has a playdate with her bestie so Austin will drop her off before heading back to the hospital. His hello is quick, followed by a goodbye as he races out the door with an excited girl behind him.

When River sees them leave, she extends her hands and wails.

"Such a Daddy's girl," Ava mumbles, then pulls out some crackers and Jell-O which instantly quiets River.

I make Ava and me some coffee from her fancy machine. Placing the steaming hot cups on the table, I sit beside her but quickly get back up again to grab some cookies from the jar on the countertop.

Their house has always felt like home to me, or maybe because they make me feel like I'm part of the family. When it comes down to who I feel more comfortable around, it's definitely Ava and Austin. I love Will and Millie, but their house has a different dynamic—way more chaotic with three boys running around.

"Tell me more about the job," Ava asks while blowing the steam away from the mug.

I quickly open the email from Meredith, scrolling to read as fast as I can. Everything is quite formal. Attached are employment forms and a contract. The pay is average compared to other roles I've applied for, but beggars can't be choosers.

My finger clicks on the third attachment, which is a job description. The main part of the role is assisting Meredith with admin-type tasks. From what I've read, nothing to do with April's stepfather, which is a relief. I much prefer working with a woman.

"I'm just a junior assistant. I'll be reporting to Meredith."

"Meredith?" Ava questions, raising her eyebrows.

"Yeah, she's Hunter Cash's executive personal assistant. I'll be helping her," I say while reading the concluding part of the email. "He's April's stepfather."

Ava shakes her head like she's in disbelief.

"Let me get this straight. Hunter Cash is April's stepfather, and you never once told me this?"

"Why would I tell you this?" I answer in confusion. "What does it matter?"

"What does it matter?" Ava repeats in a high-pitched tone. "Have you seen Hunter Cash?"

"Actually, no. He hasn't been home. April warned me her parents aren't around much. They got married about a year ago. She said their marriage is kind of weird," I blurt out, then continue so Ava will leave me alone. "I've met April's mom. Let's say she fits well into the bored housewife image."

"And you haven't met Hunter Cash?"

"No, Ava," I drag for the millionth time. "I told you, I haven't met him. He's been traveling or something. I don't know. April said chances of me running into him would be incredibly slim hence why it was okay for me to stay there."

Ava takes a moment to process, so I assume Q&A time is over.

"So, wait a minute. Let me get this story in my head in order," she begins with, slowing down like she's trying to solve a riddle or something. Then, she continues, "You're staying in Hunter Cash's house. Now, you've got a job as an assistant for Hunter Cash."

"Ava, for the love of God," I raise my voice in frustration. "Yes, I'm technically staying in his house. I'm not working for him as his executive assistant. Any more questions? Because I really don't understand why your brain can't compute this."

"I have one more question," she adds while I let out a groan and fall back into my chair. "Have you googled him?"

"No..." I answer slowly. "Why would I google him? I just figured he was like some old dude. I know he's thirty, but that's old."

An obnoxious laugh leaves Ava's mouth. "Firstly, thirty is not old. Thirty is hot. Why don't you google him right now? You're welcome."

Just to get her off my back, I open my search engine and type in his name. The page instantly fills with images of a very attractive man. As I look closer, he looks exactly like the man inside the elevator. The one with the big feet.

Oh shit...

Hunter Cash busted me staring at his crotch. FUCK! Now, how am I supposed to face him? Sure, it's one thing to see him in the office, which is manageable if everyone stays professional. But what if April is wrong, and I run into him at her house?

"Okay, why the face? He's hot, right?"

"Um, sure. Attractive, yes."

Ava rolls her eyes at me. "You sound like Mom when she's in front of Dad."

I take a deep breath, then sputter the truth. "I kinda saw him in the elevator and had no idea who he was. One thing led to another and..."

"*What do you mean one thing led to another?*" Ava almost shouts. The volume of her voice causes River to stop mid-cracker and stare at her mother in bewilderment. "You hooked up with him?"

"God, no! He just caught me staring at him."

Ava clutches her chest, releasing a long-winded sigh. "You had me for a moment. Look, not the best first impression, but it's not that bad. It could have been a hell of a lot worse."

"How was I supposed to know it was him?" I ask defensively.

"You google him. You google everyone," Ava states, crossing her arms. "At what point did you think to not google him? Your bestie says you can stay with her and her rich stepdaddy. Weren't you the least curious if he was hot?"

My gaze fixates on Ava, wondering how we're so alike most of the time, but other times, it's like we live on different planets.

"I don't know what sick and twisted world you live in, but why would I google her stepdaddy? Even the word step-daddy is just wrong."

Ava huffs, staring at me like I'm an idiot.

"Open your eyes, Alexa. Hunter Cash is hot. He's like the next biggest billionaire or something like that." It almost feels like I'm being disciplined by a teacher. "I'm sure if you ask Will or even Dad, he'd know who he is."

"Yeah, sure, I'll ask Dad," I mumble.

Ava pulls River out of her chair, wiping her down quickly.

"Back to my room. This changes everything."

Once again, we're standing inside her closet, but this time Ava pulls clothes off the rack and forces me to take them. With Hunter suddenly in the picture, everything is low-cut or short. I don't exactly have big breasts, yet Ava made sure all the blouses and bodysuits have low cleavage.

"I don't know what you're trying to do," I say while eyeing a lacy top that is not professional. "But I'm not going to dress slutty just because he's hot."

"So, you admit it?"

"I never denied it," I mutter, annoyed with her and desperate to leave. "Look, I want to make an impression and keep the job so I can earn some money to make it on my own. Not everyone was born with a silver spoon in their mouth to which they gladly eat from."

Ava places her hand on her hip, annoyed at my analogy. As far as she's concerned, her success is *all* her.

But we all know the Edwards name can get you places, no matter whether you want it to or not.

My arm is weighted down by all the clothes Ava has added. "I think there's plenty for me to choose from. Just one more favor?"

"What?" she questions impatiently.

I put on my biggest smile. "A ride home, pretty please."

On the twenty-minute car ride home, Eric calls Ava with an emergency. When he says anything is an emergency or even crisis, it's never life or death.

It turns out that when his dog walker was walking his dog, she stopped to chat with another dog walker. The dogs basically had sex while they were gossiping about something, and now Eric's dog is knocked up. The other dog's owner happens to be a long-lost ex of Eric's, and shit has hit the fan in his house over custody of the puppies.

I couldn't make this stuff up even if I tried.

Ava eventually gets him off the phone when we turn into the street of April's property.

At the front gates, I see a familiar car. On closer inspection, I notice it's mine. *What the hell?* Mom steps out of the car, looking tired. Ava stops the car near the gates, allowing me to get out.

"Mom, what are you doing here with my car?"

She moves closer to me, dropping her eyes to the ground before raising them to meet mine. Standing so close to her, I can see they're red with dark circles around them. My stomach begins to churn, thinking of how much I'm hurting her. Something I always overlook when I'm so angry with my father.

"Alexa..." she manages, keeping her voice low, "... I don't ask for much. I never ask for much. But please, this time, I'm asking you to think of me."

"Mom, I—"

She holds out the keys to my car. "I need to know you are safe. Please take your car back. I know this was a gift from your father and me, but I'm asking you to please understand how much I worry about you. I'm not sleeping, Alexa. You're my baby, and if anything happens to you..." She trails off, choking on her words.

It's time for me to stop being selfish, not if it means I'm hurting her.

"Mom," I whisper. "I don't like seeing you like this."

"Then please, take your car back. This is not the safest of cities, and I just want to know you have at least this basic necessity."

She's still holding out the keys, which I stare at for the longest of times. I may have told my father this wasn't my battle, but it's not Mom's either.

"Okay, Mom," I say faintly as I take the keys off her. "Thank you."

Her pained eyes meet mine, followed by a relieved smile. She doesn't hug me or offer any other affection, turning her back to walk to Ava's car.

It dawns on me Ava must have known, or else how would Mom have gotten home?

"Mom?" I call again, forcing her to stop and turn back around. "I love you. That will absolutely never change, okay?"

She nods silently, still with a smile on her face. "Ditto, kid."

THIRTEEN

CHARLOTTE

The passenger door closes behind me as I watch Alexa stand beside her car.

She stares absently at her keys before taking a deep breath, then squeezes the keys tight in her hand.

The engine starts as soon as she's sitting inside, and slowly pulls away from the curb and toward the wrought iron gate. The property looks very secure, requiring Alexa to punch in a code. When the gates open, she's quick to drive through without looking back.

A heavy sigh escapes me, prompting Ava to rest her hand on my shoulder with concern.

"Are you okay, Mom?" Ava asks gently.

I nod in silence, but truthfully, I have no idea how to feel anymore.

Over the years, I've watched and experienced Millie, Ava, and Addy all transition into adulthood. It wasn't always easy, Millie being the most challenging, given her affair with Will at such a young age. Nevertheless, we made it through, and I'm proud to have raised three girls into strong women.

Yet, with Alexa, things are different. I never expected to be in this place, watching my daughter walk away, knowing she carries a pain she chooses to keep to herself. It was easy at first to blame it on hormonal changes and being a typical teenager who rebels against everything their parents say, but the longer this behavior of hers has gone on, the more I think it's something bigger than I ever imagined.

I knew from experience at a young age, or maybe even the same age as Alexa, how time passes quickly, and you're forever jumping in and out of your comfort zone. One minute you're in high school, and the next, you're falling in love with your bestie's married older brother.

Those first loves are powerful. They stick with you no matter what. Alexa's relationship with Cole was nothing out of the ordinary. Two typical teenagers doing what kids their age did. Nothing appeared out of sorts from the outside, not that I'm comparing what they had to Lex and me. Alexa seemed unphased by their breakup or over her decision not to attend college.

Deep in my heart, or perhaps it is mother's instincts, something isn't right.

"Something with Alexa is not right," I confess aloud, still staring at the now-closed gates. "Watching your daughter go through something she doesn't want to talk about makes me feel absolutely helpless."

Ava nods in agreement, then releases a breath. "I understand, Mom, but Alexa is a big girl. She's trying to make it on her own. You know she's stubborn, much like you and Dad."

"Something's not right, I know it." We both stare out the windshield in silence. River is sitting in her chair quietly while playing with the dolls in her lap. "Maybe, all we can do is be here for her. I know I've offered, but I guess she's not ready, or maybe she'll never be ready."

"It's hard being young, especially in her generation. Breakups, for example, aren't like back in your day," Ava informs me, then continues. "Social media places enormous pressure on young people to paint this perfect life."

As I think back to when Alexa changed, she became much more reserved and to herself in her senior year. It wasn't just her personality, but even the way she dressed changed.

"I don't think it's the breakup. Alexa changed in senior year. Almost like something happened. I just don't know what."

Ava shrugs, pursing her lips. "Probably something at school if we're being honest here. When you're in senior year, it's all about school, right? You know, it's not easy being the daughter of Lex Edwards. There are a lot of people who have opinions about being a billionaire's daughter."

"We never wanted any of you girls to be treated differently," I tell her with a heavy heart. "It's why we did our best to keep our home life as grounded as possible."

"I know, Mom," Ava assures me. "People think it's great to have rich parents, but often it comes with being teased more than anything. Jealousy is a powerful trait."

I tilt my head in confusion. "What are you trying to say, Ava?"

"I'm saying that when I think back to high school, you got bullied if you were a rich girl with a hot daddy. Not me. I stood my ground." Ava cringes, then shakes her head in disgust. "I'm not saying Dad is hot either, but other people thought he was, is, you know what I mean."

This doesn't make sense. Alexa is such a strong-willed

girl. Growing up, she had no problem speaking up. I started to think of legal cases where bullying or harassment was part of the problem. If I focus on the victims' traits, Alexa somewhat aligns with them. However, she hasn't shown signs of taking her own life or substance abuse. Nothing that extreme.

"Alexa, bullied? Have you seen her argue with your father?"

"Yeah. It's one thing to argue with Dad, but bullies are relentless," Ava reminds me with a frown. "Cole was also hot. Girls wanted him. Alexa had what teenage girls would deem the perfect life."

All of what Ava says makes complete sense now. As I think back again to Alexa before she left for Europe, River begins to fuss. Ava begins to drive out of the windy road and toward home. When we arrive, Lex's car is parked near the door as she pulls into the driveway.

We argued last night over Alexa and haven't spoken since. The argument led to him sleeping in the guest room and me lying in bed crying. I cried until I fell asleep, then forced myself to wake up this morning and log in for work. By the time I even made it down to the kitchen, Lex was gone.

"Listen, it might not be best to come in. Your father is—"

"You're fighting over Alexa. I get it, Mom. If Austin was acting like Dad, I'd be reacting just the same as you."

"Your father is stubborn."

Ava places her hand on top of mine. "If anyone can make him see he's being an asshole, it's you."

"Maybe," I say wistfully. "Look, I have tomorrow off, so drop the girls off. I want to spend some time with them. In fact, they can stay over. My workload is much lighter this week."

Ava leans over in a rush and hugs me tight. "Mom, you're a lifesaver. These girls have been driving me—"

"Crazy?" I interrupt with a grin. "I know, been there, done that."

We finally say goodbye, and it feels good to at least be able to help one daughter who I know has been struggling of late trying to juggle it all.

Inside the house, there is nothing but silence. I suspect Lex is in his office, given it's too early for him to stop working for the day. Rather than go find him, I head to our bedroom for a shower. Given the long day, I can't be bothered cooking and decide on takeout, which I rarely do. All of a sudden, I'm craving a greasy pizza, New York style.

My phone buzzes inside my hand with Adriana's name flashing on the screen.

"I'm ordering pizza if you want to come over," I quickly tell her.

"Uh, no. Did you anger the beast?"

My lips press tight to avoid rolling my eyes. "More like the beast angered me. You know, the same old argument over Alexa. I saw her today and gave her car back."

Adriana lets out a long breath. "Good. I know she was trying to make a point, but safety comes first. I feel much better knowing she can get around."

"Me too," I breathe with relief. "Sure, you don't want to come over?"

"I'd love to, but Eric is coming over and wants to prep me for the Botox appointment."

"Oh, good luck." I laugh. "Let me know how you do."

"Will do, and by the way, you're my in case of emergency," Adriana informs me. "You know, just in case this goes wrong."

"Why not Eric?"

"He's been admiring my house way too much. I'm scared he won't try to revive me and attempt to move in with Julian."

"I wouldn't put it past him." I chuckle softly this time. "Okay, call me tomorrow. Love you."

"Love you too."

I kick off my shoes and drag myself to the shower, hoping the hot water washes away this very long day. When I step out, feeling much more relaxed than before, I throw on some bed shorts and a tank top to head to the den so I can order pizza.

Halfway through my dilemma of cheese versus pepperoni, Lex clears his throat at the doorway to catch my attention. My eyes glance toward him, ignoring how sexy he looks in his gray trousers with a matching vest. The sleeves of his white shirt are rolled up to his elbows, showcasing his toned arms and olive skin.

Why does he look extra sexy when I'm mad at him?

"Did you want me to make something for dinner?" he asks, keeping his tone neutral.

"I'm actually ordering pizza right now," I mumble, turning away. "Do you want some?"

"Sure, I'll just shower and change."

He turns around, leaving the room and allowing me time to place the order. I decide on both toppings since I'm being indecisive. The app tells me the pizza should be delivered in thirty minutes.

I turn on the television and channel surf for a bit to pass the time, settling on a renovation show. I quickly grow bored and answer emails on my phone so I don't fall too behind when the girls come over tomorrow.

Lex enters the den again, this time showered and changed into gray sweats plus a white tee.

Jesus Christ... turn away, now.

He sits beside me quietly, placing his phone on the coffee table.

"I'm sorry about last night," he says softly. "I shouldn't have argued with you over our daughter's safety, no matter how much her actions anger me."

I let out a sigh. "All we do is fight, Lex."

"I know."

"I don't know how long I can fight with you."

Lex straightens his shoulders in a panic, cocking his head to stare at me profusely. "What are you suggesting?"

"I'm telling you, I'm exhausted."

Silence falls between us until he grabs my hand and brings my wedding band to his lips.

"I can't lose you," he whispers.

"Lex," I call softly. "We need to let Alexa live her life and get through whatever she needs to. But you need to promise me something?"

"What?" he questions, his tone defeated just like mine.

"When she needs her daddy, he's going to be right there holding onto her tight."

Lex's chest rises, then falls, followed by a winded breath. "Charlotte, I promise. After all, she is our baby."

"Always." I smile.

And for the rest of the night, we enjoy our pizza and each other's company, something we haven't done for the longest time.

It reminds me of when I was eighteen, and he was Adriana's college-aged older brother. How we spent hours laughing and fooling around, thinking we had our whole lives ahead of us and our love would stand the test of time.

Well, it did.

Some things in life are destined to change, but being in love with Alexander Edwards will never be one of those things.

FOURTEEN

ALEXA

My first week on the job was *exhausting*.

There was so much to learn, from policies to procedures and computer systems, plus learning everyone's name. It got to the point where I played this game in my head to try and link someone's face to their name. Like the man who looks like Brad Pitt, but his name is Jeffrey. So, every time I interacted with him, I'd sing this stupid song to myself about Brad Pitt working for Amazon, only to get to the part where Amazon reminded me of Jeffrey.

Like I said... exhausted.

My brain is overloaded, working extra hard to retain all the information so Meredith doesn't think I'm incompetent.

For the most part, Meredith is fine to work with. She's straightforward with her instructions, always thinks one step ahead, and has her shit together. It's easy to see why she's an executive assistant. Her organization skills are next level.

The hours are longer than expected, not that Meredith forced me to stay back. I just thought it would be smart to catch up on work when no one was around. The office is large and always chaotic with people going in and out of meetings. Plus, there is always some celebration in the kitchen, which I don't mind so much because it means cake.

Late hours mean leaving here close to dark. Thank God Mom gave me the car back because, without it, I'd be riding the bus late at night with strangers.

Two weeks pass, and things become more routine and less daunting. Colleagues' names aren't so hard to remember anymore. Most of them are older college graduates with degrees. They are nice enough but being the youngest is always hard, like I needed to prove myself. *Story of my fucking life.*

Josh, from IT, invited me to one of the events in Malibu next week. I suspect he has a thing for me since he keeps asking me out to lunch. He's cute, sure, but workplace romances or flings seem like a super bad idea. Eric made sure to inform me of that the day I started work. It came with a spiel that started something like, "Suits are the devil's playground..."

It's Monday morning. According to Meredith, it's the monthly board meeting, so she got in early to start preparing. She gave me a list of tasks, all of which are manageable and nothing too out of my comfort zone. As I sit at my desk with my head down, Monica, one of the ladies in finance, pops by to say hello.

"You ready for the meeting?"

I glance up and smile. "I've prepared everything Meredith has asked me to do."

Monica shakes her head with a grin. "No, I meant, are you ready for the meeting? He's back."

"Who's back?"

"Hunter," she whispers while leaning in. "But people call him Mr. Cash."

"Oh, I'm not going to the meeting."

"Of course you are. Your name is listed as an attendee."

Confused by what Monica says, I open the document with the attendee's list and see my name. I don't know how I missed it before, probably because I was so busy doing other things.

"You're right," I mumble, followed by a wave of panic. "I've never met Mr. Cash."

Monica nods with a knowing smirk. "Well, aren't you in for a treat then."

Without saying another word, Monica leaves, prompting me to rush to Meredith's office, which is beside Hunter's. Mr. Cash. *Shit, what do I even call him?*

My knuckles tap on the door, then Meredith looks up.

"Um, Meredith, you never mentioned me having to attend the meeting," I mention, trying to hide my panic.

"Mr. Cash only requested it this morning."

"Oh, he did?"

"Yes," Meredith answers, removing her glasses to wipe them, only to place them back on again. "Is that a problem?"

"Uh, no," I mumble.

I turn back around, wondering why I'm so nervous, but I manage to busy myself with work until it's time to join everyone. Thankfully, I wore a very presentable blouse and skirt, yet I decide to wear my blazer, not sure what board meeting attire should be.

All the things I need are in my hands—laptop, notebook, pen, copy of the agenda printed out, and my phone. Taking the deepest of breaths and giving myself a much-needed pep talk, I walk to the boardroom to join everyone.

Inside the room, four men are already sitting at the

table. Monica quickly enters, smiling at me before taking a seat. I look at her in a panic, not sure where I'm supposed to sit until she motions with her head to move toward the back of the room.

Meredith enters next, taking a seat right at the front, which is next to Mr. Cash. She glances at me from the front before making her way toward where I sit.

"You'll be responsible for recording the minutes of this meeting. Try to record as much as you can," she instructs, straightening her shoulders. "The meeting will be about three hours. Please help yourself to the refreshments, beverages, or anything offered during the meeting."

My mouth opens to ask a question about the minutes, but she walks away as quickly as she walked over here.

The boardroom fills up within minutes, with almost all seats taken apart from the important one at the front. About twenty people are in the room, making it far less intimidating than before.

"Please stand for Mr. Cash," Meredith announces.

Everyone in the room stands up, so I follow, but my curiosity gets the better of me. I glance at the door as Mr. Cash walks in. His greeting is simple, just a "Please sit" before he gets himself settled. How bizarre Meredith requested everyone stand like he's the king or something.

Today he's wearing a navy suit without a matching vest. His white shirt is buttoned down, showing a small area of his chest. I can't help but stare, blaming Ava for putting thoughts in my head. *Fine, thirty is not so old if the person is hot.*

Then, his eyes dart to mine, forcing me to smile politely from nerves. He doesn't smile back, instead turning away to talk to Meredith. I swallow the lump in my throat, wondering why he would insist I join this meeting if he can't even smile politely.

The meeting drags on for what feels longer than three hours. Each department has its turn of speaking, mainly numbers and projections. Occasionally, Mr. Cash voices his opinion, to which no one disagrees.

Jeffrey smashes the finger sandwiches, and Monica stares at the little cherry tarts for the longest time before eating three in a row. I try not to focus on anyone else, but boredom finds me when a heated debate starts about subscription fees, and I assume the argument shouldn't be part of the minutes.

Mr. Cash calls for the meeting to end, wrapping up with a speech about what he expects to see next month.

As everyone chatters while exiting the room, I pack up my things to follow. Meredith walks over to me with an unusual expression. I'm not sure what it is. A mixture of confusion and worry.

"Alexa, Mr. Cash would like to speak to you privately."

Confused, I tilt my head. "Did I do something wrong?"

"No," she's quick to answer. "He has just requested to speak to you once everyone leaves. Please stay back."

"Um... okay," I stammer.

My heart begins to race like I'm running a marathon, making it hard to do simple tasks without my limbs turning to Jell-O. I think back to all the times there have been confrontational moments, but oddly, they mainly involved my father.

Then, I think, if I can go up against Lex Edwards, to which many people have tried and failed, I can go up against anyone.

Okay, calm the fuck down. You don't even know what he wants.

With a deep breath, I gather my things and walk toward where he sits. Meredith is standing next to him but leaves as I get closer, shutting the door behind her.

It's just us alone in the boardroom, making it all the more intimidating. Mr. Cash glances at me with the same expressionless look as before.

"Please sit," he commands.

I place my belongings on the table, then sit where Meredith was sitting during the meeting.

"I'd like to formally introduce myself," he begins, extending his hand. "Hunter Cash."

My hand reaches out to him, and as our skin touches, the warmth of his sends a sensation throughout me which catches me by surprise. Instantly, my thighs press together as the unknown feeling stirs. *Blame Ava.*

His chestnut-colored eyes continue to watch me. With a courteous smile, I pull back my hand and place it on the table, ignoring my now sweaty palms.

"Alexandra Edwards," I introduce myself in a rush, realizing it was rude of me not to say anything during the handshake. "I'm Meredith's assistant, but I guess you know that."

"I am always aware of what goes on inside my office and more importantly, at my company."

"Of course," I say with a forced smile. "It makes for a successful entrepreneur and CEO."

He tilts his head with a curious gaze, making me regret what I said. I hate that my father's influence has stuck with me over the years. Some things are hard to forget.

"An interesting observation..." he simply replies, "... especially from someone as young as yourself."

My lips press together, not wanting to say anything else, especially about my family. I'm sure the internet reveals my identity, but as far as I'm concerned, I won't be mentioning it unless asked directly.

"Thank you."

Great, what kind of a response is that? Sweat forms on my back, causing my blouse to stick uncomfortably to my skin.

"I guess there's no tiptoeing around the subject matter," he begins as I hold my breath, praying I don't have to talk about the fact that I'm an Edwards. "April has informed me you're staying in my house."

How stupid of me to forget. My shoulders relax, grateful my family is not the subject at hand.

"Yes, she kindly offered. I promise it's not for long," I ramble, not taking a breath. "I should be gone soon once I find a new place to stay. Hopefully close to the office."

Mr. Cash, Hunter, shit, he hasn't even told me what I should call him.

"April is welcome to have friends stay."

"And your wife," I continue, with a nervous energy. "She's lovely, Mr. Cash."

The second I call him formally, his expression stiffens. Unsure why, my eyes drift to his hand resting on the table. He clenches a fist, almost as if my calling him Mr. Cash angers him.

"My wife," he strains, gritting his teeth. "Is anything but lovely."

Oh great, now what have I stepped into? Surely, my big fat mouth could have been kept shut. I think of ways to segue out of it, again, learning much-needed lessons from my father.

"She's been nothing but accommodating and lovely to me," I tell him, trying to steer the conversation. "With all due respect, Mr. Cash, I have all these minutes I need to email out. Is there anything else you need me for?"

His eyes meet mine, our gaze locking in uncomfortable silence. I can't deny he is incredibly sexy. He has that whole chiseled jawline going for him which means his face appears very masculine. As for his hair, it's a mousy brown color and slicked back, styled like he's modeling for an Armani campaign.

I've always been turned off by the older-man thing, given that Cole is my age, but thirty ain't so bad. Maturity is all of a sudden sexy, and I find myself squeezing my thighs shut again at the thought.

God, what fucked-up rabbit hole are you falling into?

"That's all I need..." He trails off, lowering his gaze to the table, but then slowly raises his eyes to meet mine again. "For now... Alexandra."

I smile politely, then grab my things with shaky hands as he watches me. Quickly, I rise from the chair, careful not to lose my balance from whatever the hell is happening to my nervous system.

Exiting the room, I close the door behind me and let out a huge breath which comes out a rasp.

As long as things stay professional inside the office, I can get through whatever he throws at me.

But as for staying in his home... I beg myself to save every penny to get out of there as fast as possible.

FIFTEEN

"Eric, is there a point to this story?"

The young man serves our drinks, prompting Eric to smile politely while pretending he's not checking the bartender out. There's an awkward silence when he leans over, but thankfully he's quick to pull back and continue to offer his services before leaving us to serve other customers.

"Did you smell him?" Eric asks, fanning himself.

"Yeah, he smelled nice. And?"

Eric cocks his head, staring at me with judgment. "I have so much to teach you still."

I shake my head in disagreement. "The last time you taught me something, it stuck in the wrong way. Never again."

"Oh?" Eric grins proudly. "Do tell."

"No chance. Besides, I told you I only have an hour for lunch."

In typical Eric fashion, he pouts when he doesn't get his way, crossing his arms like a petulant child. Though, also like a child, he soon forgets, then brings up something else with excitement.

"Spill all the juice about Hunter Cash," he begs with way too much enthusiasm. "I need to know everything."

Eric isn't the right person to discuss my brief encounter with Hunter Cash. Nor is Ava, despite her abusing me over text messages. What am I supposed to say anyway? There was a stupid moment when I shook his hand, and something weird happened. How that night when I was attempting to fall asleep, my brain wandered into uncharted territory, thinking about what it felt like to have an older man touch me.

The more I think about it, the more juvenile it sounds, or at least, the more juvenile it makes me sound. All I have to do is play this whole thing down and show Eric that Hunter has no effect on me whatsoever.

"There's not really much to say," I answer nonchalantly. "I met him last week in a board meeting. He was polite, but that was it. I really don't have much to do with him. Actually, I don't have anything to do with him. All the work I do is mainly for Meredith."

"That's not what Ava tells me."

"Ava knows nothing," I retort, realizing it made me sound guilty like I've done something wrong. "I meant to say that Ava is a bored housewife making up shit. There's nothing to tell."

Eric keeps his gaze fixated as if he's attempting to break me.

"So, you don't want to tell me Hunter Cash is bestie's stepdaddy?"

An unflattering groan escapes me. "You sound just like Ava. What's the big deal? Yes, he is technically April's stepfather. End of story. Can we please move on to something more enjoyable and entertaining to talk about?"

"Sure." Eric grins in amusement. "How about your upcoming birthday? It's the big two oh."

I somewhat regret changing subjects now. "Let me guess. You want to have a party of some sort?"

"Honey, it's not a birthday without a partay," Eric claims. His eyes light up, which I know is not going to be a good thing. "What are you thinking? Destination birthday? Something at home?"

I'm quick to interrupt him. "In case you have forgotten, a certain father of mine doesn't talk to me. So, home is out of the question."

"Not the best of my ideas," he acknowledges, tapping his finger on his lip. "How about a dinner somewhere fabulous?"

"I'd rather just keep it low-key."

"Low-key is no fun. Besides, you kept it low-key last year and the year before that."

"How do you know I kept it low-key last year?" I question him with a frown. "Just because you weren't there in Mykonos doesn't mean I kept it low-key. Now when I think back, it was far from low-key. I don't think I've ever been more drunk than I was that night. Thanks to April, of course."

"This April," he drags, rolling his eyes. "I must meet her. Find out what all the fuss is about."

I place my hand on Eric's. He's such a jealous dramatic friend and doesn't like it when he thinks someone is stealing his thunder.

"April is chilled," I say gently. "As for my birthday, let me get back to you. It's not exactly on my mind right now."

"Oh, yeah?" His eyes dance mischievously. "Is there a certain gentleman occupying your thoughts?"

"I wish. I feel like I've been without a boyfriend forever."

"You have been without a boyfriend forever," Eric reminds me so easily. "Look, honey, I get the whole I don't need a man thing, but kitty needs to eat. You know what I mean?"

"Eric, I always know what you mean. For once, I agree, kitty is hungry." The moment it leaves my mouth, it comes across as all wrong, making me cringe. "That sounds incredibly wrong. There's this one guy at work, Josh, but you said don't shit where you eat."

He nods eagerly. "Workplace romances can be so hot. You know, that whole enemies-to-lovers thing."

"Okay, but Josh is not mean, so there are no enemies to lovers."

"Fine, friends to lovers. My point is, workplace romances can get super awkward, especially when it doesn't end well."

"I've been invited to some work function. It's no big deal like some client party out in Malibu this weekend. I'm kind of thinking of going, you know, just to show some team spirit."

"Yes, yes, yes!" Eric claps his hands. "Wear something hot, not too slutty, but enough to show everyone you're fun outside of work.

"I'm thinking jumpsuit, maybe long sleeve, plus wedges.

"Virgin-white jumpsuit," he insists.

"Sure," I jest, even though the term virgin-white is unsettling. "I'll see what I can find."

As Eric excuses himself to use the restroom, I quickly check my phone to see if there's anything important I've missed. He takes longer than expected, not giving me much time to get back to the office. As I grow bored, I check my Insta DMs to see the messages I've left unanswered. When it comes to social media, I'm the worst offender unlike everyone else in my generation who posts everything. Lately, I just can't be bothered. It's all a bunch of bullshit anyway. All the photos people put up are fake or filtered. Everyone is trying to sell a lie they live.

Inside my inbox is a message from Beau that he sent over two weeks ago, and I forgot to respond to it. From memory, I was on the bus and then got a call from Meredith about the job.

I read the message again, unable to hide my smile. It won't surprise me if Beau is sleeping with his professor by now.

ME

> You do know my father's name is also Alex Edwards? At least, that's what he used to be referred to as. Guessing you've found your way into your professor's pants. Or she found her way into yours?

Eric walks back from the restroom, prompting me to put my phone away so we can leave. Judging by the look on his face, something must have happened in the restroom, but as always with Eric, some things as better left unknown. Once you hear something, it's *very* hard to unhear it.

"Thanks for lunch, Uncle Eric," I tease.

He shudders in his expensive Dior suit. "Please don't. Until I wear man pads and a cane to walk, Eric will suit me just fine. Actually, Big Daddy might work. Lex seems to like Charlie calling him that."

I slap his arm without hesitating. "You promised to behave."

"Sorry, Big Daddy promises to be on his behavior... next time, okay?"

I'm dressed in the so-called virgin-white jumpsuit, not that I look like a virgin, or maybe I do. Who knows anymore? I wonder if it's possible to be revirginized since the chances of it happening to me are quite high.

The sleeves of the jumpsuit flare at my wrists, making the low-cut cleavage not seem as noticeable. The jumpsuit looks quite plain as I glance in the mirror, so I grab a belt just to accessorize. My hair is left loose in soft waves down my back. It's been a while since I've cut it, but I don't mind the length so much.

My makeup is simple, just a little wing eyeliner, nothing too dramatic.

April enters the room, throwing herself on the bed. We haven't seen each other much since she got a casual job working at a studio lot.

"Oh, you look hot, mama." She whistles, admiring me from the bed. "Maybe I should come? Find some hot guy in Hunter's office."

I turn around from the mirror. "I think I need to get laid."

"Wow," April shouts while sitting up to rest on her knees. "You're admitting you're human and not a robot?"

"Funny," I sneer. "Eric pointed something out the other day. He's right. It's been forever since I've had a boyfriend. I'm not craving a relationship or anything serious, but I do miss having a guy around. Is that bad?"

"No. Why do you put this pressure on yourself, Alexa?"

I shrug. "Things with Cole became so intense too

quickly. I think I've just been scared to experience another relationship like that."

"But every relationship is different." April restyles her hair, placing a bun on top of her head while she speaks. "I don't have a ton of experience, but every guy I've been with has been different. It doesn't hurt to play the field a little."

"Maybe," I mumble, letting out a long-winded breath. "If it happens, it happens. Just not tonight. I don't exactly want to mix business with pleasure."

April throws her head back, laughing. "In an outfit like that, I won't be surprised if you bring a guy home."

"I'm good." I grin, then finish putting my hoop earrings on. "Do you think you can give me a ride to Malibu? I can Uber it back. I just don't want to risk anything, you know, if I have a couple of drinks."

"Um, are you forgetting that we're no longer in Europe?"

It only dawns on me now my drinking days are over, at least for another year until I turn twenty-one.

"Shit, you're right. I didn't even think about that," I say, lost in thought. "God, sometimes I just wish we could go back. So much freedom, the responsibility here is so much more."

Since drinking isn't possible, I don't see any reason for April to drive me. That is until I attempt to start my car, and it makes a funny sound. Of course, my luck, it has to happen tonight. I end up having to ask April again for the favor and just plan to Uber it back. April doesn't mind since she plans to meet an old friend in Santa Monica with the possibility of crashing there.

With my purse ready to go, April drives me to Malibu. The event is being held by a major client of ours. A lot of people from the office said they would attend, except

Meredith. She didn't do work events unless Mr. Cash asked for her attendance.

When we get there, April waves goodbye after I exit the car. Taking a deep breath, I put on my best smile, knowing if I want to make an impression and keep my job, being social gives me the best chance.

Thankfully, Monica is here as well as some other people I'm somewhat friends with.

"Alexa," Monica calls from where she's sitting at a long picnic-style table. I wave with relief, then walk over, glad not to be alone. "Happy you made it."

"Me too," I respond politely.

"What are we having to drink tonight?" she asks, even though all the girls at the table already have a drink in hand.

I don't want to sound like a party pooper, but don't want to get anyone into trouble.

"I, uh, can't exactly drink."

"Why not?" Caitlin, one of the girls from marketing questions. "Oh my god, are you pregnant?"

"No," I blurt out, then look down at my stomach. "Why? Is it the jumpsuit?"

Caitlin and Monica laugh in unison. "It's just this thing when new girls start. They kinda know they're pregnant but hope to secure a job. You know, cause firing a pregnant woman is so frowned upon. We have bets because it's happened way too often."

"Right, I had no idea," I muse, then smile. "I'm not twenty-one."

Monica places her arm over my shoulder, bringing me in for a hug. "Well, I'm twenty-one times two. I'll get you a drink."

Before I have a chance to tell her it's fine, I can drink a mocktail or even soda, she's left for the bar. It's not overly busy, so she returns soon after with a colorful-looking drink. It looks like juice of some sort with a bit of red, plus mixed fruit floating at the top.

Taking a sip, I try not to make any facial expressions from whatever alcohol is mixed into the drink. A few more sips and it becomes delicious enough, given the sweetness of the pineapple juice, but I try to pace myself.

As Caitlin tells us a story about this guy she met on Tinder last night, Monica orders more drinks to make the night more enjoyable.

Between the warm sea breeze and good company, I relax and enjoy the atmosphere. We laugh at all the gossip circulating in the office until the CEO of the company holding this event makes a quick speech. He thanks everyone for attending and makes sure to end by wishing everyone an enjoyable night.

I suck on my straw, emptying my second glass so easily. This time, Adeline, the other girl sitting with us, fetches the round of drinks. Monica appears to be too wasted already, singing loudly to the song playing in the background.

"So, have you met Kevin from the mailroom?" Adeline asks once she returns. "He's notorious for delivering big packages."

Monica and Caitlin fall into a fit of laughter. Even though I haven't been formally introduced to Kevin, I have walked past him once or twice, and the only thing I noticed was his big biceps.

Caitlin is sitting across for me, but suddenly, her laughter fades, and her eyes widen. She's staring directly at me, causing me to tilt my head in confusion from the sudden change in demeanor. She purses her lips as if to warn me of something, but my reflexes are slow from all the drinks. As I turn behind me to look at what she's glancing at, my stare hits a body a few inches away.

My eye level, from sitting down, is to the belt buckle of the pants in front of me. I lean back against the table, slowly drawing my eyes up until they meet Hunter Cash. Everyone at the table sits up straight, all with a smile on their drunk faces.

"Good evening, Mr. Cash," they greet in unison while I sit here silently.

"Good evening, ladies," he responds with a friendly smile, nothing at all like the cold-hearted CEO inside the boardroom. "It looks like you're enjoying yourselves."

The girls nod while on their best behavior. If only he had heard Caitlin telling everyone how her Tinder date wanted anal on the first meet-up or about Kevin's large package.

Unlike the suit I've seen him in, his attire is slightly more casual. Navy dress pants, a white buttoned shirt, and tanned-colored shoes. *Why is he so sexy? Cocktail talking ... just the cocktails... plural.*

His eyes fall upon me as a smirk plays on his lips. God, they look so... don't say it.

"It's nice to see you are fitting in well with the team, Alexandra."

How he says my name triggers something inside me, or maybe the multiple cocktails. Either way, I start to feel dizzy, but I do my best to come up with something intelligent.

"Thank you," is all I manage to say.

You idiot.

"Well, I'll leave you ladies to it. Enjoy yourselves."

As he walks away, Adeline leans forward, almost

tipping a glass over. "Why does he have to be so hot? I swear, I can't get anything done when he's in the office."

"Argh, me too," Caitlin complains.

Monica laughs. "I can get a lot done, which is why I was promoted to finance manager. My husband wouldn't be happy if he knew I was thinking dirty things about my boss."

"Fantasies," Adeline corrects Monica. "Fantasies are healthy. Ask Alexa. She's young and hot too."

"What do you think about Mr. Cash?" Caitlin puts me on the spot.

"Old," I admit, not wanting to say he's hot in case it somehow leaks to him. "I mean, he's older than me."

"Yeah, he is older than you. But do you think he's sexy?"

"Of course, he's attractive, but not my type. He's not my age, so I'm looking for a guy my age."

Monica grabs my hand. "I have a brother."

"Oh, here we go again," Adeline drags. "Monica has been trying to set her brother up with everybody."

"What's wrong with him?"

Monica purses her lips. "Nothing is wrong with him. He just lives with my parents still."

"Enough said." I cringe, then continue to ask, "Wait, how old is he?"

"He's graduated from college," she simply replies.

"Okay, well, that's not so bad."

"He's also into Star Wars," Monica adds.

I pull a face again until Caitlin yells out, "Hey! I like Star Wars."

"Is he a hot geek?" I question with trepidation.

Monica lets out an exaggerated groan. "No, my sisterly due diligence is over. Why don't we go dancing? I need to burn off all these cocktails, or my husband will kill me since we're visiting his parents tomorrow."

There's a band playing music in the corner. The beat is funky, a few songs I recognize, and a few I don't. Until we got up, the dance floor was empty. Then, people joined us, and before we knew it, the space was full.

Josh makes his way to where I am dancing, and it's only polite I dance with him. He's a good dancer, plus smart enough not to put his hands on me at a work event.

As we continue to dance, my eyes accidentally fall upon Hunter, who is standing with some people I don't know. He is staring directly at me, so in a panic, I turn away, suddenly feeling self-conscious.

For the rest of the night, I try not to look at him and enjoy the music. When the band calls the last song of the night, we make sure to dance our hearts out, but then the lights come on.

Out of breath, I place my hand on my heart. Josh leans over to suggest going somewhere else.

"I'd love to, but it's late. I should get home."

The girls interrupt the awkward moment just to say goodbye. I make my way up the wooden stairs, almost stumbling on the last step.

My hand reaches into my purse to retrieve my phone. The screen turns on, bright and blinding me, but I still manage to find my Uber app. There appears to be a shortage of drivers, fuck.

"You need a ride home?" Josh asks.

Suddenly, he's next to me again.

"Um, no, I'm good. There's a driver—"

"It won't be necessary, Josh," a deep voice behind me says. "I would much prefer if I took Alexandra home."

I turn around swiftly and stare into Hunter's eyes. Or is

it Mr. Cash? Argh, my head is spinning. *Stop overthinking everything.*

"It's really not necessary for either of you to take me home. I can manage an Uber."

Hunter juts his chin, then raises his brows. "I take my employee's safety very seriously, Alexandra. So, I insist on taking you home. End of the story."

Josh steps back, intimidated by Hunter's command.

"Of course, Mr. Cash." Josh touches my arm gently, a gesture Hunter notices. "See you on Monday, Alexa. We'll do lunch?"

"Sure, sounds good." I smile.

As Josh begins to walk away, Hunter's expression shifts. He looks angry, which makes no sense. I could ask him what was wrong, but I barely know the guy. The thought of being alone with him in the car is already awkward enough.

"I'm honestly fine to wait for an Uber," I tell him one more time.

Hunter grabs my hand to cross the street, catching me by surprise.

"I'm your boss, Alexandra," he states firmly, releasing his grip on my hand when we reach his car. "Just get in the car. I'm taking you home."

SIXTEEN

Hunter's black Aston Martin is exactly like my father's.

My mouth opens to mention it but quickly snaps shut, not wanting to get into a discussion about my father, of all people.

"Nice car," I point out while Hunter opens the door for me in a gentlemanly manner. He motions for me to get in, looking very impatient. "But really, an Uber could have easily picked me up."

Hunter rolls his eyes, annoyed at me for stating the obvious again. "I'm driving you home."

There's no point in arguing, so I sit inside the car. The first thing to catch my attention is his scent. The smell of a masculine aftershave mixed with the leather seats is intoxicating. My head leans against the headrest as I close my eyes for a moment, knowing all these feelings circulating around my body are all to do with the alcohol and nothing else.

Nothing else.

Hunter gets in and starts the ignition before the engine

roars upon taking off. The drive home is not too far from Malibu, but being in close proximity to Hunter Cash makes it even longer.

The roads are dark and windy, and the silence is much more uncomfortable than it needs to be. Soft music is playing, but I feel obliged to say anything to start a conversation.

"You really don't have to drive me home," I mention. "I planned an Uber because April dropped me off. My car was doing this weird thing, and I'm not exactly a mechanic, but I'm sure it has something to do with the battery. It kind of sucks because I wasn't prepared to be without a car."

I continue to ramble on as if I'm chatting to myself since my talking is better than nothing.

"I'll probably have to go tomorrow to get it looked at. I don't even have a mechanic. All these kinds of things, my family normally did for me." As soon as it comes out of my mouth, I instantly regret it. "Anyway, it was a nice function tonight. I really enjoyed myself. Everyone at work seems so nice."

Hunter still hasn't said a word, and I'm all out of small talk as we turn the corner, still in silence.

"Look, I'm not a small talk person, so that's cool if you want to sit here in silence," I continue to speak, even though I just gave him the option to not talk at all. "Look, if you're annoyed I drank, sorry. I know I shouldn't have. Please don't get angry at the girls.

It's just I—"

Hunter quickly interrupts me, "Alexandra, you don't need to explain yourself. You had fun tonight. That's all that matters."

"So, you're not pissed off that I was drinking, and I'm technically underage?"

"Yes, you are underage for drinking. One more year. You are turning twenty soon, am I correct?"

"How did you know that?"

"Because you're an employee. As I said, I know everything that goes on in my company. It's important I have the right people under me."

My lips press together while I think about his last comment.

"I thought you didn't get involved in hiring. I thought it was all Meredith?"

Hunter tightens his grip on the wheel as he takes the corner fast. The speed jerks my body toward him, forcing me to grip the door for support.

"I guess when a certain Edwards applies for a role at your company and stays in your house, it's nice to know a little more about them, don't you think?"

I let out a shallow sigh. "Look, I don't particularly want to talk about my family. I'd rather people in the office don't know who my father is."

"I don't understand, Alexandra. You are the daughter of Lex Edwards?" he questions in a condescending tone. "What's there not to be proud of?"

"As I said, I don't particularly want to talk about it."

Hunter doesn't press or ask any more questions, falling into a digestive silence for the remainder of the drive.

Thankfully, we pull into the familiar driveway as I breathe a sigh of relief. When we exit the car, Hunter enters the code to open the big glass doors. The lights are off, but upon our entering, they turn on, sensing us.

"Thank you for the ride." I scratch the back of my neck, trying to ignore the awkward tension between us. Thank God I'm somewhat still buzzed because this could be way worse if I wasn't. "I guess I'll see you in the office on Monday."

He places his car key in his pocket, staring at me oddly.

"Hunter," he says out of nowhere as we walk in. "You can call me Hunter."

"Okay..." I stammer. "Hunter, it is. In the office, would you prefer it if I called you Mr. Cash like everybody else?"

Hunter rubs his chin with his hand, and the familiar smirk lingers on his lips. "Mr. Cash in the office is fine."

"Well, since we're talking about names, you can call me Alexa. No one calls me Alexandra unless I'm in trouble."

"Alexandra is a beautiful name. I'll stick to calling you that," he insists.

My breath catches in my throat. I find myself unable to move, paralyzed on the spot, then I realize my silence has dragged on too long.

"It's fine. You can call me Alexandra. If that's what you want, Hunter."

"That's what I want," he answers in a strangled voice but then clears his throat. "At least, for now."

My lips flatten thoughtfully before I turn my back and walk down the long corridor toward the guest wing. I've wondered which room he sleeps in, assuming it's upstairs. Aside from April's quick tour of the home, I've never gone up. April's room, or should I say suite, is not far from the one I'm staying in. So, Hunter and Kathy's room must occupy most of the second level like a penthouse or master quarters.

Inside my room, I shut the door behind me and lean against it trying to catch my breath. My heart is beating like a drum, unable to slow down in pace.

Out of nowhere, my head begins to spin from a combination of my night with Hunter and the multiple cocktails consumed at the party. To try to avoid being hungover tomorrow, I head to the bathroom for a quick shower.

I lingered way too long under the hot water, my fingers turning into prunes. When I finally get out and brush my teeth, I remember to take painkillers to avoid waking up with a headache.

My hands rummage through my bag, then drawer, but come up empty. Not wanting to go to the kitchen this late, I decide to just climb into bed instead. Whatever happens tomorrow can be tomorrow's problem.

It's late, yet I'm far from tired. Hoping to find something to help me fall asleep, I reach for my phone on the night-stand to find something to watch.

The home screen has notifications from the group chat with my sisters and cousins. There's message after message, and the last three lines said something about babies, losing my interest.

I click on my Instagram to notice the red arrow noti-fying me there are unread DMs.

BROMANO

Nice of you to reply promptly.

My fingers type quickly to respond.

ME

Some of us have lives, you know.

The typing bubble appears, even at this late hour. Considering he's on the East Coast, it would be five in the morning.

BROMANO

Why are you awake? I assume someone who has such a busy life needs her beauty sleep.

ME

I was at a work function. You know work, right? Something you do when you want to earn money.

BROMANO

Really, I had no idea, so you landed yourself a job, huh? Do I dare ask exactly what job you are working at this hour in the morning?

ME

Lucky I'm still drunk, or I'd take offense to that comment.

BROMANO

Naughty girl, underage drinking. I hope you're behaving yourself.

ME

I'm always the good girl, unlike you, the bad boy.

BROMANO

If only you knew Alexa.

ME

I'm glad I don't know, player. Anyway, I need to get my beauty sleep.

BROMANO

Of course, princess.

A grin spreads across my face, but it's soon followed by a yawn. Placing my phone back on the nightstand, my eyes begin to fall heavy in need of sleep.

My mind goes in and out of consciousness.

All of a sudden, I'm naked in bed, and Hunter is kneeling in front of me.

"Have you been talking to another man?" he questions in a jealous tone. *"Because you belong to me, do you understand?"*

Hunter doesn't give me a chance to respond, entering me whole as I moan in delight.

"Good girl." He places his hand on the base of my neck, almost choking me.

A loud rasp leaves my dry throat as my chest is rising and falling, trying to slow down my breathing to a normal pace.

What the hell was that dream?

My head pounds, and I quickly realize it wasn't such a good idea to go without taking any painkillers. Nor is it good to have a dream about fucking a man so off-limits.

I manage to sit up in bed for a moment before laying back down as my head spins. An involuntary groan escapes me, and I'm unable to get comfortable with the continuous throb near my temple.

"Fucking hell," I complain to myself, deciding to go find some pain relief in the kitchen.

It's probably a good five-minute slow shuffle before I get across the entire house to the kitchen. When I get there, I'm reluctant to turn on the lights as it's such a big kitchen and someone might see me. I stumble my way to the pantry, hoping to locate some Advil. I know the last time I was in here, I discovered a first-aid box. Scanning all the shelves, I try to remember where I saw it.

"Are you looking for something?" a voice behind me asks.

I jump back, clutching my chest, unable to breathe. Turning around, Hunter is standing at the entrance, half exposed with no shirt on. My eyes gravitate toward his stomach, counting every single abdominal muscle cut to perfection. His low-cut black and red checkered bed pants hang low, showcasing the V which some men are known for. I shake my head to rid myself of impure thoughts, but it makes me more unsteady on my feet. Then, I remember my dream. My stupid subconscious is trying to sabotage my waking life.

"I was looking for something. I have a headache."

"You do know what cures a headache, don't you, Alexandra?"

I'm not sure if it's my mind going to places it shouldn't, but it's thinking something dirty and totally not shareable in the confined space.

"Advil?

A smirk lingers on his lips. "Yes, one of many things."

He reaches across me, almost trapping me in the corner, to grab a box. His arm brushes against mine, causing a jolt of electricity to shoot right through my body. I'm standing here barefoot in my boxer shorts and tank, quickly realizing there's no bra beneath. I cross my arms, trying to cover myself, the move catching his attention.

"Hangover already, I assume," he notes in dark amusement.

I nod, but the movement feels like a jackhammer running through my head.

"I should've said no," I groan, pressing my forehead. "I live in regret."

"You were having fun," Hunter points out, but then his expression turns wary. "Is Josh bothering you?"

"Josh? He's nice," I respond honestly. "He asked me out to lunch and stuff, nothing big."

"I don't look fondly upon workplace romances."

"It's not a romance." I almost laugh, though my head

says don't you dare. "I'm not interested in him if that's what you're inferring."

"I'm just making sure you understand I do have some rules."

As he hands me the Advil, I reach out, but the box falls to the ground. Great, hungover, and clumsy. I reach down to grab the box at the same time he does, but our hands touch accidentally.

The jolt shocks me again, causing me to whimper. I quickly swallow, refusing to look at him, knowing whatever I'm feeling right now is dangerous.

Repeat, Hunter Cash is April's stepfather. I work in his company and sleep in his house. It's wrong, forbidden, and the only reason why I'm feeling this is that I'm so desperate to physically connect with a man again. That's it. Maybe any man will do.

I hear his own strangled breathing inside the small space, only inches apart. His hand extends to pass me the box, forcing me to gaze into his eyes to say thank you.

"Thank you," I whisper, mesmerized by the eyes staring back at me. "I should probably go back to bed."

"Of course."

He helps me on my unsteady feet as I try to stand up. Once again, his grip on my hand lingers much longer than necessary. Unknown to him, I catch his eyes staring at my chest with a pained gaze.

My throat makes a sound, shifting his attention, but I turn around to leave the room. Suddenly, I stop in my tracks, turning back to face him.

"Do you actually live here?" I question out of curiosity. "Why haven't I seen you around?"

"I'm here when I need to be here," he responds bitterly. "Anything else?"

The change in mood leaves me annoyed. Why does such a simple question goad some sort of reaction from him? Surely, a simple yes or no would suffice. But no, he turns into a jerk.

If he wants to act like one, I'll torture him just as badly.

"Nope, I guess I'll head back to my room to take care of my headache."

His eyes narrow, knowing his mention of what cures headaches is directed at orgasms. Since I don't have a guy, it looks like only I can cure my headache.

"You're playing with fire," he says in a low, grumbling tone.

"And you're married," I remind him. "Or are you only married when you want to be?"

Hunter lowers his eyes to the floor. "It's not what you think."

"I have no idea what to think."

"Don't you have a headache to take care of?" he asks, changing subjects to avoid discussing this weird arrangement between him and Kathy. "It's late."

"You're right. Good night again, Hunter."

A sly smile forms on his lips. "Good night, Alexandra Edwards."

SEVENTEEN

The sun basks on my face forcing me to wake.

A begrudging groan slips out of my mouth, and simple tasks like opening my eyes become all too much. Turning my head, I bury my face into the silk pillow, attempting to fall back to sleep.

That is until the memory of last night comes flashing back.

"*Argh...*" I complain again.

After returning to the room, I'm ashamed to admit I took things into my hands. I can't remember the last time I'd done it, nor come that quickly. The truth is, my head is not pounding, and Hunter's advice worked.

Maybe, I should thank him.

Yeah, sure. How awkward would that be?

Unable to sleep any longer with my stupid thoughts, I lean over to grab my phone, only to knock it over onto the ground.

"For fuck's sake," I mutter, attempting to half-hang over the bed to retrieve it. This weekend is not starting off to be the greatest, not to mention I still have the issue of my car.

Considering I'm trying to save money to get my own place, throwing money at a stupid car is going to set me back.

As I lay back down, there's a text message on the screen, but I don't recognize the number.

> **UNKNOWN NUMBER**
> Your car is fixed. Just in case you're wondering why it suddenly starts.

> **ME**
> Who is this?

> **UNKNOWN NUMBER**
> Is that how you talk to your boss?

My eyes widen when Hunter reveals it's him, but I can't help but grin, then feel guilty for doing so.

> **ME**
> Technically, I don't report directly to you. However, I can be on my best behavior, Mr. Cash.

> **HUNTER**
> You're dangerous...

My stomach flutters reading his message. So, I didn't imagine things last night? Surely, I'm not that naïve. He is a man, a man with needs. I'm a woman, a young one at that.

Though he has a point, this is dangerous. I don't know how to respond, but I have to before this escalates.

> **ME**
> Thank you.

Shit! Why did I hit send so quickly? Why has no one invented an unsend option yet?

ME

I meant to say thank you for fixing my car.

Have a good weekend.

The text messages end. At least, he doesn't respond. My last message sounded stupid, especially if I ran into him somewhere in the house. I pull the bed sheet over me, wishing to crawl into a hole and die.

With a sense of urgency, I grab my phone again with this urge to google him. Quickly typing his name, the screen fills up with results within seconds. Most of what appears are articles on his company, stuff which bores me. There's nothing on his personal life except for his grandfather and his passing about two years ago.

I switch to images mode, but it's mainly pictures of him in a suit. Frustrated, I abandoned my search, unsure of what I was looking for.

My finger taps on my phone, dialing Millie's number. I need perspective, and if anyone can give it to me, it's my sister who fooled around with a guy ten years older than her.

"Alexa," she greets. "What's up?"

"Are you home?"

"Yeah, Will took the boys to watch some baseball game."

"Great," I tell her. "See you soon."

Millie's house reminds me a lot of Mom and Dad's house. There's a more homely feel, herringbone floors, and white furnishings even though she has three boys. It's that Hamptons vibe, unlike Ava's place, which is much more modern.

"How's the new job?" Millie asks, placing a fruit platter down between us.

"It's good, challenging, but I'm managing."

"I'm glad to hear. First corporate jobs are massive learning curves. Still, I was lucky to work at Mom and Nikki's firm."

"Yeah." I nod, picking on a piece of melon. "So, can I ask you something?"

"Anything."

"When you first started having feelings for Will..." I slowly speak, but then rephrase my question. "I mean, when you started looking at him differently, did you think it was weird because he was older than you?"

"Of course," Millie tells me, her emerald eyes bright as she fondly remembers their past. "It felt wrong, you know. I was still kind of going out with Austin, and feelings for Will just started to take this turn. I'd always looked at him like some older cousin, then all of a sudden, he's this sexy man in a suit who I imagined doing dirty things to."

All of what she said is exactly how I feel right now. The only difference is that he wasn't her boss or bestie's stepfather. I do remember when Dad found out about Will. They were in New York, and Addy was back home with me. Addy said Mom told her she'd never seen Dad so mad in her entire life. It makes sense. You find out your business partner is screwing your young daughter behind your back.

"You tried to talk yourself out of it, right?"

"Many times," Millie confesses. "I felt like some dumb kid with a crush. Will was more experienced. You know, he was adulting with Dad."

I stare at the table, then release a sigh. "Please don't say anything to Ava, promise?"

"Promise."

"Hunter, I mean Mr. Cash." I shake my head to gather my thoughts. "There's this weird tension between us."

"Oh," Millie mouths. "I see."

"Nothing has happened. It's just..."

"I get it, I really do. Alexa, just be careful. He is your boss, right?" She questions then I nod. I'm not at all offended by her warning since Millie is a logical thinker. If this was Ava, she'd be telling me to take my clothes off and report back. "And isn't he married?"

"Yes to everything. I knew you would give me the reality check I needed."

The back door opens, and all three boys come running in, covered in dirt.

"What happened?" Millie asks in shock.

Will lets out a huff. "There was a swing incident. Someone fell, another one tried to rescue him, then they got knocked over into the dirt."

Millie crosses her arms. "How do you explain your third son?"

"He just thought it would be fun to play with his trucks in it." Will rubs his face with his hands. "I'll take the car later to the car wash. You should see the inside."

"Boys," Millie yells. "Straight in the bath."

Millie disappears to bathe the boys, leaving me with Will. The morning must have exhausted him since he makes himself a coffee and adds three shots to make it super strong.

I've watched over the years as their family dynamics have changed. I truly admire them for adopting Ashton, given the circumstances of Will sleeping with Ashton's mom when he and Millie were broken up. In the end, Ashton deserved a family who love him, and he's so lucky he has that.

Even though it's chaos in this house, Will and Millie just make it work. They also make it look so effortless, which I know it's not. Three boys are three boys. I was tired from looking at them run around with endless energy.

As for Will and Millie's age gap, no one would even know. Will looks young for his age, and Millie is more mature, so it somewhat evens out. They're both career-driven but also put their family first. They remind me so much of Mom and Dad.

"I heard about the new job," he mentions while the coffee is brewing.

"Yeah, news travels fast in our family..." I trail off to then remember my father. "Does my father know?"

Will rubs his chin. "What answer will make you happy?"

"He knows, doesn't he?"

He simply nods, then removes his glass mug from the coffee machine and leans against the countertop.

I press my lips flat. "Was he mad?"

"Unless you go to college, always assume he's mad."

"Of course." I sigh, wishing things were different. "So, you're a CEO and all in the know with business. What do you know about Hunter Cash?"

Will drinks his coffee, thinking carefully before he speaks. Something he's good at doing.

"He's innovative and has some great ideas on the future of media."

"And that's it?"

"What else would you like to know?"

I shrug. What else did I want to know? Like, how is Will supposed to know about Hunter's personal life?

"He's married to April's Mom, who is five years older

than him. She had April at a young age," I begin with, then continue. "But they don't kinda spend time together."

A knowing smirk graces Will's lips like he knows something.

"Okay, why the face? What do you know?"

"There's been talk of his marriage being of convenience," Will reveals.

"I don't understand?"

"Hunter inherited a lot of money from his grandfather. Some believe his grandfather had a clause. To access the inheritance, he needed to marry."

My brows furrow in confusion. "That sounds like a plot to a bad movie. People think this?"

Will simply nods. "Trust me. It's not unusual. Old people think marriage is the only thing one should do in life, even if it's with the wrong person."

"How much money are we talking about? Because if what you're saying is true, then there must have been a large pot of gold waiting at the end of the rainbow."

"An extraordinary amount," he suggests with a sneer. "His grandfather inherited a large sum from his own father. They owned farming land in the South. I might be mistaken, but Hunter was raised by his grandfather. I'm not entirely sure about the parents."

When I think back to my conversation with Hunter, he was very dismissive when it came to talking about Kathy. As for Kathy, she was living her best life by spending money. April said their marriage was different, but she never asked questions and just went with the flow.

It makes sense if, in fact, what Will said is true.

"Hey, can I crash here this weekend? I'm happy to take care of the boys tonight if you want a date night or something?" I offer, just to avoid going back home and running into Hunter.

"You're always welcome to stay here. You know that," Will assures me as Millie walks back into the kitchen. "Hey, how about a date night tonight?"

Millie tilts her head in confusion, then glances at me. "Babysitter?"

I nod, with a grin, then put more fruit on my plate.

"God, yes," Millie cheers. "Dinner without anyone interrupting us."

"You know, I can stay here until Monday morning. I can watch the boys if you want to go away for the night."

"Don't tease me," Millie drags.

"I'm serious." I laugh. "Look, I babysat before. Mom and Ava aren't far if I need help, but trust me, I got this."

"I know, but—"

Will interrupts Millie. "I'll organize the plane now. Palm Springs, just you and me, baby."

Millie purses her lips to then break out into a smile. "Okay, but don't get too excited. I have my period. Sorry, sis. I know... TMI."

I laugh, poor Will.

"But your mouth is okay, right?" Will questions with a serious expression.

Millie smacks his arm. "You're such a guy!"

I have spare clothes and my toothbrush in Millie's guestroom, and she says it's fine to borrow work clothes for Monday. This way, I avoid going back home.

As for the boys, when they found out it was just me for the weekend, their eyes lit up, and they didn't care their mom and dad would be gone.

Aunt Alexa is apparently the funniest aunt ever, according to them.

I'll take the challenge. Anything to forget about Hunter Cash.

At least for this weekend.

When Monday rolls around, I find myself in a much better headspace. Playing Pokémon all weekend does that to you.

The boys were well-behaved, enough that I didn't need to call for backup help. Mom video called to ensure everything was okay and even offered to come over and cook, but I had it all under control. Dinosaur nuggets for the win.

Running into Hunter at the office is inevitable. I brace myself for it, but he is traveling out of state, according to Meredith.

"You must be relieved when he travels," I mention, careful not to raise any concerns on her end over my questions. "Gives you a break, right?"

"Not really. Mr. Cash was scheduled for meetings this week inside the office. All of a sudden, he changed his schedule so now he is away. If anything, it's more work for me."

"I'm sorry."

"My dear." Meredith smiles politely. "Why on Earth should you be sorry? This is my job."

"I know you like things organized," I rush, trying my best to lie even though I wonder if his disappearance has anything to do with Friday night. "If there's anything I can assist with, please let me know. I'll just get back to my reports before lunch."

As I leave her office, Josh catches me in the corridor and reminds me about lunch. I happily accept since it's at the café downstairs.

The week passes with no sign of Hunter. No text, no email, or anything, like he disappeared off the face of this earth. At home, April mentioned he was home on Sunday for a bit and mentioned traveling again.

I didn't pry, not wanting to raise suspicion.

Eric insisted I still celebrate my birthday next weekend. Surprisingly, I'm excited to turn twenty. Maybe people, in general, will take me more seriously since I no longer have the word 'teen' attached to my age.

The plan for my birthday involves some Japanese restaurant where they throw food at you. To be honest, I'm surprised Eric suggests this since he only ever dresses in designer clothes. Imagine his Gucci silk shirt being ruined in a food toss, the outrage of such a disaster.

As much as dinner would be nice, I want to do something more fun.

"You've come to the right person." April grins as we sit in the den and finish binge-watching *Gilmore Girls*. "Oh, do I have plans!"

I chuckle, digging my hand into the bowl of popcorn. "I'm excited. Should I get bail money ready?"

"Nah, but what are the chances of you wearing leg warmers?"

"In the California heat? Zero."

April doesn't say another word as we both argue over which guy Rory should have ended up with in the show.

The week drags on, so when Friday finally appears, I breathe a huge sigh of relief. There are a few more reports I need to email out before I call it a day and start the weekend. Mom wanted to spend some time with me, suggesting breakfast tomorrow. Apparently, Dad is in Atlanta for some work thing with Will and Uncle Noah.

Saturday night is a birthday party of an old friend from

school. I wasn't too excited to go, but since no one else from school was invited, I accepted not to be rude. As for Sunday, I planned a much-needed day by the pool to soak in the sun and finish the book I'd been reading.

"Alexa, may I speak with you?"

Meredith motions for me to follow her to the office she uses. Closing the door behind her, she requests I take a seat.

Her tone sounds cold like I'm in trouble or something. I start to panic, given I can't afford to lose my job.

"There's going to be a change in your workload next week."

"Oh, really. What's the change?"

"Mr. Cash, as you know, is quite a busy man. The company is in the middle of acquiring a few businesses. There's a lot of work involved, and Mr. Cash has requested you assist him."

She stares at me avidly, waiting for me to respond, but I don't understand what is happening.

"I don't understand, Meredith. I'll be assisting Mr. Cash with what exactly?"

"Mainly project work. Any tasks he might need," she adds, keeping her tone professional. "If Mr. Cash thinks you're up for the job, then Mr. Cash thinks you're up for the job."

"What if I don't think I'm up for the job?" I state, panicked. "I've only been here for, like, what? A month. I've only just learned how to work with you."

"I'll be here to assist you should you need anything."

"But what about you? What about the help you need?"

"Alexa," Meredith calls softly, removing her glasses. "I'll be okay. I'll always be okay. It's your turn now. Show him what you can do."

I continue to sit here, speechless.

"Enjoy your weekend. I'll be heading off shortly. My sister is coming to town, so I must be home when she arrives."

From the bits and pieces Meredith has revealed about herself, she is married but has no children. She said it's why she's able to dedicate her time here since her husband likes to fish, and she doesn't.

"Okay," I muster up while standing. "Have fun with your sister."

As I walk out, the panic is suddenly replaced by anger. Why would Hunter change my job after what happened on Friday? I pull my phone out and send a text.

ME

Why did you change my job?

HUNTER

That's no way to talk to your boss.

ME

I don't understand why you must make this more awkward.

HUNTER

I don't understand why you think there's something to be awkward about. Is there something you want to share, Alexandra?

I don't know how to respond. He's playing some game to which I don't know the rules in order to play fairly.

At home, I check my bank balance to see how much I've saved. The only places I found that I could afford to rent were run-down studios in very questionable neighborhoods. If my mom found out, I'm pretty sure she'd have a heart attack.

All I need is to save for another three weeks, and I should be able to afford something nicer.

Problem solved.

Three more weeks of living in Hunter's house. After that, he has nothing to hold over me.

Nothing at all...

EIGHTEEN

"So, what's the problem?"

Ava is sitting beside me on her third mimosa. About an hour ago, she played rock, paper, scissors with Millie. Whoever won gets to drink. The loser is in charge of the kids.

Of course, Ava came out as the winner, lucky to be lying in the sun enjoying our lazy weekend.

"The problem is I don't want to work for him," I complain, letting out my millionth annoyed huff since I found out yesterday afternoon.

"Sounds to me like he wants to get in your pants." Ava's giggles are followed by a hiccup. "Too bad he's married."

I glance at Millie, who presses her lips flat and doesn't say a word on the matter. Since our conversation at her house, she hasn't brought up the subject again.

"Ava, can you be serious for like a second?"

She crosses her arms. "Fine, go on."

"I was thriving in a job reporting to a woman. I don't do well when being bossed around by a man."

"You have daddy issues, like literally," Ava concedes.

"You've always argued against whatever Dad says or rules he's set. On a positive note, your many battles with Dad mean you've got the stamina and strength to go up against Hunter should you disagree with him."

"He's my boss. It's different. I need money."

The boys become loud and rowdy, forcing Millie to threaten them if they continue. It's no popsicles after the pool, something they desperately want so quickly behave.

"The real question here is..." Millie begins with, then continues, "... is this what you want to do long term? If you're in this to make money for a greater dream, then just be professional so you can move on to your next goal."

I shrug, then release a sigh. "I don't know. I just want my own place. As for a career, it doesn't spark anything in me. It's just a job."

"Take it from me. You have to love what you do," Ava assures me.

Millie nods. "I've always wanted to work in law. Maybe because I watched Mom, and she looked like such a badass winning all these cases. It's like fighting crime but being a law-abiding citizen at the same time."

"You know, you always told Millie and me you wanted to fix sick people." Ava smiles, then continues to sip on her Mimosa. "You made us call you Dr. Edwards."

"I was just a kid..."

"Not all dreams have to change," Ava says wistfully. "But back to your problem, don't let Hunter get to you. Work hard, prove yourself, then get the hell out of his house before something happens."

Ashton jumps into the pool, splashing all three of us. I let out a gasp from the cold water, but maybe it's the wake-up call I need.

Ava is right. Work hard, prove myself, and make sure nothing happens.

"Nothing will happen," I assure my sisters. "Trust me."

Monday mornings have become my least favorite part of the week.

I avoided going back to April's the past weekend again, this time crashing at Ava's house. The fear of running into Hunter gives me this constant paranoia. Everything needs to stay professional.

I'm standing inside his office, waiting for him to arrive. He's an hour late, so I return to my desk and try to answer emails.

"Mr. Cash is here," Meredith informs me.

Great.

Hunter turns up whenever he feels like it, and I'm supposed to stop everything just for him. Taking a deep breath, I fix my blazer and then follow Meredith to his office. He briefly glances up, then drops his gaze back to his phone.

"Meredith, please train Alexandra on how to complete the Anderson report. I'll also need all the contracts printed, signed, and emailed to James Peterson's legal team."

"Of course, Mr. Cash."

"You may both leave."

I draw back, wondering why he is acting like a rude asshole? Following Meredith out of his office, I expel an annoyed huff but keep my opinions to myself.

The entire day is spent completing the reports he requested. When I finally finish, I print all the contracts and am forced to go see him to get them signed.

I knock on the door, waiting for him to gesture me in.

"Come in."

With the pile of contracts in hand, I place them gently on his table, not throwing them in his face as much as I'd love to.

"For you to sign," I simply state.

Hunter reaches out for his pen, then goes through each tab to sign the pages required. He closes the contract and places his pen down on his last page. This is bullshit. Like seriously, Meredith could have done this in two seconds. It is part of *her* role.

"Do you have a problem, Alexandra?"

I cross my arms, staring into his smug face.

"I don't understand why Meredith couldn't have done all of this for you?"

Hunter diverts his attention back to his screen while I stand here waiting for him to respond. There's an email open, but he quickly closes it like it's top secret or something.

"Do you think it's wise to question your boss's decision?"

"Probably not," I tell him. "But I think we crossed being wise when you told me to make myself come when all I wanted was some Advil."

His eyes widen as his fist clenches on the desk. Then, he glances at me with a stern expression.

"And did you?"

"Did I what?"

"Did you make yourself come?" he questions, still not showing any emotion like I'm supposed to answer his question honestly.

I clear my throat. "I have work to do."

Leaving his office in a rush, I sit at my desk, ignoring my

heated skin and possible flush of my cheeks. I avoid looking in the mirror because if they are, my looking at it will make it ten times worse. My water bottle sits at my desk, and I drink a decent amount to cool myself down.

Then, I think to myself, if you want to make me uncomfortable by forcing me to work with you, I'm going to strike when you least expect it.

An hour later, two clients arrive to meet with Hunter. As Meredith has taught me, I greet them in the foyer and walk them to Hunter's office. Opening the door, I guide them, prompting Hunter to stand and shake their hands.

When he's busy with the small talk, I quickly pull out my phone and send a text to him.

ME

Yes, I did.

The ping of his phone catches his attention, so he motions for the two gentlemen to take a seat.

"Is there anything else you need, Mr. Cash?" I ask, faking my best smile.

He glances at his phone, and I almost instantly see his chest hitch. I wait for him to look at me, then when his gaze lifts, I can see his eyes burning with desire.

"Nothing right now, Alexandra. I'll be sure to call you when I need you."

I step outside, fist-pumping myself mentally, but then realize that whole stay-professional boat has sailed.

I'm grateful he is busy with clients, giving me time to get work done with the hope of getting out of here before he summons me to do other shit.

The office is scarce. Only a few people left. I have one more thing to do then plan to leave as well. Josh asked if I wanted to join him at some bar his friend was playing at. I agreed since hanging out with him is not so bad, plus I have nothing else to do.

Inside the copy room, I'm cussing at the photocopying machine. I'm sure there's a place in hell for machines such as this. The paper jam is driving me crazy. I let out a groan, ready to kick the machine. Besides, who would see, anyway?

Suddenly, a hand reaches over me and presses a button, making the paper come out. The scent of aftershave forces me to close my eyes, but I quickly open them, not wanting to fall under his wicked spell. His body is only inches away from mine, but given we are in the copy room, it doesn't look good if someone sees us.

I clear my throat. "Um, thank you."

"Maybe you should turn around and explain to me why you would send me such a message right before a three-hour meeting?"

Taking a deep breath, I slowly turn around. His eyes are blazing as if he is trying to control himself.

"You asked me a question, and I thought it was rude of me not to answer. You know, I'm supposed to respect my boss."

"Alexandra," he grits, biting his lip. "I asked you to work for me because I think you have the potential to go far in this company."

"Oh, really?" I drag, not letting him say anything else. If arguing with my dad has helped me with anything, it's standing up to men who think they can get what they want. "And here I thought you just wanted to sleep with me. Anyway, I need to go now. You know, I'm young and single. I got myself a date tonight."

I attempt to walk past him, but he grabs my arm. "Don't play games with me, Alexandra."

"I could say the same to you."

"Who are you going out with?" he demands rather than asking politely.

"A man," I tell him, refusing to succumb to his intimidation. "But it would be extremely unprofessional of me to tell my boss what goes on in my personal life."

He releases his grip, then places his hands in his pockets, trying to calm himself down. I have no clue why he's so angry. It could be because no woman challenges him. He's always used to getting what he wants.

"I don't appreciate you lying to me."

I tilt my head, drawing my brows. "There's nothing to lie about. I have a date, and it may or may not end in having sex with him. That's all there is to say." I check my phone, pretending to look at the time. "I better not be late. Have a nice night, Mr. Cash. I'm sure your wife is expecting you to come home."

Tossing my hair behind my shoulders, I walk out and don't turn around.

After sending the contracts out via email, I pack my things and head home to get changed. Josh said the venue is kind of posh, so I opt to wear a black bodycon dress that sits just above midthigh, pairing it with my hot pink strappy heels. My hair is left out in waves again because I can't be bothered doing anything with it.

April walks into my room, eating an apple.

"Love it," she cheers. "This is your getting laid outfit."

"Josh is nice, but I'm not going to fuck him..."

The moment it leaves my mouth, there's a knock on the door. April's mother, Kathy, walks in wearing an elegant gold gown. She's a very beautiful woman, appearing to age very well.

"Well, don't you look darling," Kathy compliments with a smile. "To be young again."

"Mom, c'mon, you look gorgeous."

I nod in agreement. "You look stunning, Kathy."

"Thank you, girls." She smiles, spinning around to show off. "It's a charity event. Of course, Hunter is running late."

My lips turn upward into a forced smile, ignoring the sweat forming in my palms. I remember what Will said, but I don't believe him. Kathy is beautiful, and Hunter *is* a man. Surely, he can see the beauty, and given she is his wife, he has to be fucking her. It's expected, given they share the same bed.

Suddenly, I bow my head in humiliation. What the hell am I thinking teasing a man like him?

"I better go," I tell them, then grab my purse off the bed. "Have a good night, Kathy."

"You too, sweetheart."

I practically race out of the room, and house, fumbling in my purse for my keys. I'm standing next to the driver's door, still attempting to find my keys which annoys me, given my purse barely holds anything.

A hand grips my arm, causing me to jump in shock.

"You're coming with me," Hunter bellows.

"Are you crazy?" I barely manage, out of breath. "I have someone to meet."

"Over my dead body."

He begins to walk and demands I get into his car. I do so but make it obvious I'm annoyed. Without even hesitating, he starts the ignition and revs the engine.

"Where are you taking me? Kathy just said—"

"My place."

It was only a fifteen-minute drive to the apartment complex, where Hunter apparently owns the penthouse. I stayed quiet for the car ride and just stared out the window.

I've been in my fair share of penthouses, given my parents own a number of them. It's nice, for sure, with windows everywhere and views of downtown LA.

The furniture is modern, but the place looks like a showroom more than someone living here.

"Nice place," I mention, looking around. "Big. So, is this your man pad? I don't understand."

Hunter places his keys on the kitchen countertop with an amused expression.

"I guess you're used to living the luxurious life. This is where I stay unless I'm needed at the house."

"Wait, so you live here?"

"Yes, Alexandra. Is that a problem?"

"It's just... your wife lives in another house."

"That she does."

Hunter pours himself a drink that looks like bourbon or something of that caliber. It's clear by his close-ended answers I'm not going to get much more out of him tonight.

I place my purse on the countertop, watching him enjoy his beverage. "So, you don't offer your guest a drink?"

"I'll offer my guest a non-alcoholic drink. I don't want you to drink and regret anything."

His liquor cabinet is right next to him. I walk over, even though it means I have to stand right next to him. There are multiple bottles, but I spot the vodka. Unscrewing the lid, I don't hesitate and take a long sip until it burns. Hunter wraps his hand around the bottle, pulling it from me. A few drops spill down my chest, dripping between my breasts.

"You're wet," he whispers.

I rest my hands on the glass table, trying to still my beating heart.

"I shouldn't be here," I tell him softly.

"But you are."

"You forced me."

"No," he states adamantly. "You could have fought harder. Not getting in the car or even downstairs you could have walked away. You want to be here, Alexandra."

"Please don't call me that," I beg.

The vodka, combined with all these desires, consumes me as I stand here trying to fight my urge to touch him.

"It is your name, is it not?"

"It's the way you say it. It makes me..." I trail off, shaking my head to free myself of these dirty thoughts.

"Tell me," he whispers, moving in closer. "Tell me how it makes you feel."

"I... I can't. You're my boss."

His finger runs down my arm, causing me to break out into goosebumps.

"Now, when you call me your boss, it makes me..."

"Makes you what?" I question, staring directly into his eyes.

Hunter clears his throat, but I see he is struggling, which turns me on even more.

"Want to cross every line possible..."

Unwillingly, I bite my lip as my body aches. Everything feels overly sensitive, and the cravings grow stronger every single second that passes.

"I won't fuck you, Alexandra. If that's what you're thinking." His admission catches me by surprise. "You're young."

"I'm twenty next Saturday," I remind him with sudden annoyance.

A smirk plays on his lips. "I know, I'm counting down the days."

And just like that, he admitted the truth. I'm young, only nineteen, and he is thirty. We're only just over ten years apart, like Will and Millie. Yet society has a stigma on age gaps.

Like I give a fuck, anymore.

"Let me get this straight." I breathe, keeping my gaze fixated on him. "You won't touch me, but I can touch myself?"

"*Alexandra,*" he grits.

I take his hand, even though I have no clue where his bedroom is. He senses my lack of direction and guides me to the room at the end of the long hallway.

There's a king-size bed in the middle with black satin sheets. All around the room is glass, meaning anyone can see us.

Oh... the thrill of being caught.

The desire is bringing out the spontaneity in me. I've never felt as turned on as I do at this very moment.

"If you won't touch me, then you can watch me touch myself."

"*Alexandra,*" he bellows, desperately trying to hold back, but it's easy to see the force is greater than he can control. "*On my bed, now.*"

His demands cause my body to react instantly. Without another word, I pretend there are no rules between us, no lines, and I lay in the middle of his bed, fully clothed.

Resting my head back, I spread my legs and slowly slide my hand over my lace panties. They're soaked, causing me to gasp at the slightest touch.

Hunter stands at the end of the bed, watching me with a strained expression. I close my eyes, listening to my body.

My hand lingers between my legs until, out of frustration and impatience, I refuse to drag this out, desperate to come.

Pushing my panties aside, I thrust two fingers inside, arching my back as a moan escapes me. When I pull them out, they glide so effortlessly against my clit. I slowly get the rhythm right, knowing I won't last long.

The bed suddenly moves, and Hunter is lying beside me. I can feel his hard cock pressing against my thigh, but he makes sure to keep a certain distance with his lips.

"Is this how you played with yourself when you thought about me last week?"

"Yes," I croak, barely able to speak.

"Good girl," he whispers. "Make yourself come for me again."

I move my fingers faster as the sensation builds, and my skin tingles in delight. When the flutter builds in my belly, I let out a loud moan as every inch of me explodes into a euphoric finish.

Unable to catch my breath, I continue to lie here with my eyes closed, but then he reaches out to grab my hand.

My eyes open to watch him place my wet fingers inside his mouth. Instantly, the ache returns, just as a smirk spreads across his face.

"Perfect..." he hums, gazing into my eyes. "Just like I imagined."

NINETEEN

The walk of shame, better described as the car ride of shame, was some Uber driver who spent the entire drive arguing with his friend via Bluetooth.

Hunter made it clear he didn't want to attend the charity event with Kathy, given he was an hour late, and his phone kept blowing up while I was lying in his bed, bringing myself to orgasm.

I didn't ask any questions, despite the curiosity eating me alive.

When he complained about having to leave, I used it as the perfect excuse to leave too. Unlike the other night, I ordered the Uber before he could stop me, though he quickly questioned me on where I was going. It was easy to see he battled with having to attend the event versus driving me home.

Frankly, I was spent, desperate to get home.

Barely able to move my limbs, I change into my pajama's and climb into bed yawning from the exhaustion of tonight. Just as my eyes begin to fall, April comes barreling into my room.

"Um, hello, Grandma," she greets in a sarcastic tone. "You do not look like someone who got laid."

My cheeks flush, so I hide part of my face beneath the sheet.

"I told you I wouldn't. I wasn't feeling well tonight, so decided to come back home."

I hate lying to April, already feeling the guilt of what I've done. If this feeling doesn't stop me from making any more bad decisions, I don't know what will.

"I almost wish I went with you just to get out," she complains, throwing herself next to me on the bed. "Mom lost her shit when Hunter didn't answer the phone."

"Oh." I swallow, forcing a concerned expression. "He didn't show up?"

"Yeah, he showed up over an hour late. I don't know what happened. I've never seen Mom so angry."

"They have, um, a weird marriage." The moment I say it, I quickly rush, "I mean, just different, I guess, to my parents."

"Like they're not madly in love with each other," April claims, then cocks her head. "I hope he treats you right in the office. He told me about how you'll report to him for some tasks."

"Yeah, nothing major," I lie again. "How often do you talk to him?"

April shrugs. "I dunno, just when I see him around and stuff. He's been home a lot lately. I'm surprised you haven't run into him."

"I've been out a lot. Speaking of which, I should be out of here soon. It's been great, but you know I can't stay here forever."

April grabs my arm, clutching it tightly. "Don't leave me. What will I do in this dungeon alone?"

I manage to laugh. "This place is far from being a dungeon. Besides, I've seen you flirting with the hot gardener. Is there something you want to share?"

April's eyes widen in panic. "What did you see?"

"What did you do?" I exasperate. "April... tell me."

"Look, he's just really good at..." April coughs and then jumps out of bed. "Stuff... involving his tongue."

"God, you're such a bored housewife." I chuckle. "I need some sleep. Goodnight."

"Nighty night." She winks before leaving and turning off the light.

I'm sitting at my desk, minding my own business, and praying Hunter doesn't show up to work. Clearly, I didn't think last night through. It's one thing to be caught up in the moment, but another to realize in the light of day decisions made under the influence of a handsome CEO will have consequences later.

Hunter arrives after lunch with a bunch of people from some company he is acquiring. He busily shows them around while I assist Meredith in preparing some materials for the afternoon meeting. At least I don't have to be alone with him.

"Is there anything else you need?" I ask Meredith while helping her put a booklet in front of some chairs in the boardroom. "I was going to work on the report you sent me, but if there's anything else?"

"Mr. Cash has requested you sit in on this meeting."

"What for?" I blurt out, then clear my throat. "I apologize. That was rude of me. I didn't sleep well last night."

"Minutes, please."

I nod, then take a deep breath. At my desk, I'm grabbing what I need for the meeting when Josh appears out of nowhere.

"Hey, you didn't show up last night?"

"Oh, yeah, about that—"

"Alexandra was requested to stay back to perform some extra work for me," the voice behind me says.

My body reacts before I can string a sentence together. How does he do this to me every time? He makes me look like an idiot, unable to say anything intelligent.

"Oh," Josh responds, forcing a smile. "I'm sorry. I just thought you would have texted or something."

"I, uh, the work Mr. Cash insisted I perform was much more than I anticipated. I was wiped out afterward. I'm sorry."

"It's cool. How about Friday night? You free?"

"Alexandra," Hunter calls sternly. "The meeting is about to start. Please make your way to the boardroom."

"I'll let you know." I smile as I walk away and enter a room full of people.

Purposely, I take a seat all the way at the back to avoid eye contact with Hunter. With all my tools out and ready to start, I begin taking notes as Hunter stands in front of the room and presents some data on the screen. His public speaking skills are excellent, much like most of the men in my life. They all have this confidence and ability to own a room with the delivery of their speeches or presentations.

As I try my best to ignore how sexy he looks today in his navy suit, he takes a seat while another woman gets up to talk about future projections. I'm busy trying to capture what she says, but my phone buzzes next to me.

HUNTER

You left me in quite a predicament last
night.

ME

Stop distracting me. Some of us are trying
to work.

I shake my head, trying to listen to this woman speak
when my head is imagining Hunter walking around with a
rock-hard cock all night long. *Shit. Don't go there now.*

HUNTER

The smell of you was all over my fingers. I
had to take things into my own hands last
night. Imagining your bare pussy in front of
me, soaking wet...

The moment my eyes read the entire message, an involuntary cough escapes me, causing everyone to turn around.
Great, now I'm embarrassed and turned on at the same
time.

"Sorry, please carry on," I tell everyone, then bow my
head.

I turn my phone around to avoid the distraction and
continue to jot dot everything Carol is saying until something catches my attention.

"Here is a list of who is dominating the market." Carol
points to the screen as everyone looks. "Harperlex Media is
currently in the first position with their new investment into
streaming sites."

Harperlex is an entity of my father's company or something like that. All I know is he owns it, amongst many
others. Carol suddenly catches my attention, prompting me
to place the pen down for a minute.

"Our team is working on a plan to move to the number one position by the end of the year."

Wait, boot my dad's company out of the number one position? Hunter glances my way for a brief moment, then back to Carol.

"Thank you, Carol," he quickly interrupts. "Ian, I'd like you to talk about staff numbers, please."

For the rest of the meeting, I do what I need to do until my hand cramps up from the in-between writing and typing. Hunter calls the meeting to an end, but Carol lingers to discuss something with him. I follow Meredith to her office and close the door behind me.

"Meredith, can I ask you a question?"

"Of course."

"Is Carol trying to ruin my dad's company?"

Meredith stares in confusion, then her expression softens. "Alexa, it's just business. Everyone is always fighting for the top spot. Granted, your father's company is always number one. I assure you, this is normal, and the industry is quite competitive."

"So, she's not like doing anything bad. She's not going out of her way to bring it down, just healthy competitive tactics?"

"Hunter is not that type of man." Meredith smiles.

I leave Meredith's office feeling better about the whole situation, then sit at my desk for the next two hours to type everything out before emailing everyone. The moment I hit send, Hunter responds to my email requesting I come to his office.

People are still in the office, making it less daunting to be alone with him. I slowly make my way over, then knock on his door.

"Come in."

Opening the door, he's exactly where he always is, sitting in his big leather chair.

"Close the door behind you, please."

I close the door but remain near the entrance. Hunter gazes at me and stands up. As he walks toward me, I back myself against the door with a racing heart. He leans his hand flat on the door, not allowing me to move.

"I want more," he demands, bringing his lips to my ear. "Right here. I want you to play with yourself."

"But... but... what if someone comes in?"

Hunter leans over, locking the door. "Satisfied?"

"People saw me come in."

"You do report to me, correct?"

I nod with a breath caught in my throat.

"Then I request you slide your fingers into your panties and show me how wet you are right now."

His words create a frenzy within me, and I don't hesitate to pull my skirt up to rub between my legs. The moment I touch my clit, an electric shock runs through me, causing me to whimper.

"Beautiful," he whispers. "Now, make yourself come for me."

Hunter angles himself in the crook of my neck, blowing soft air as I rub myself to the brink of a blissful finish. Biting down on my lip, I struggle to keep quiet, so he places his hand over my mouth.

"I don't want anyone to hear you come for me. Only I get to see you or hear you like this, understand?"

With his hand placed firmly against my mouth, I still manage to nod until the orgasm consumes me, and my eyes shut tight to ride the intense wave.

My chest hitches, trying to catch my breath as he slowly removes his hand.

"You're driving me crazy, Alexandra," he whispers. "If only I could do the things to you I want to do."

"So..." I breathe, trying to calm down. "Why don't you?"

He watches his thumb glide against my bottom lip. "Because there's no turning back once I do."

Hunter's reluctance to touch me leaves me annoyed. What does he expect me to do? Make myself come every single time? I've been doing that for years.

"I guess that's your loss." I fix my panties and drop my skirt. "I've had my fun. It's a shame you can't too. If you'll excuse me, I need to pack up to go home."

As he steps back, I unlock the door, making sure no one sees me. Thankfully, everyone is distracted wishing Jennifer in admin a happy birthday. There's a cake, and usually when there's cake, the whole office flocks to it.

A few emails came through during my time away, so I quickly answer them, but one, in particular, wanted a report which took forever to download.

After a good thirty minutes, I've once again gone over my usual finish time. Annoyed, I grab my things and head to the elevator. Pressing the button, it eventually arrives, so I enter and head toward the back as the doors close.

Then, they spring back open, and Hunter enters.

Fuck. Okay, be strong.

When the door closes, the elevator moves as we stand in silence until he reaches over and hits the stop button.

"Henry, in the control room, has fifteen minutes on his break," Hunter informs me as he moves closer. "I'm done waiting. I want my turn."

A smirk lingers on my lips. If he wants his turn, I will give him a taste of what it's like to do all the hard work himself.

My hands rest on his chest as I feel his heart beating fast.

"On your knees," he commands. "Mouth open."

I follow his demand, getting on my knees while opening my mouth as instructed. Slowly, I raise my eyes to meet his, and he unbuckles his suit pants and releases his cock.

The pool of wetness between my legs spreads everywhere, admiring how perfect his cock is. Hard, long, and the perfect angle to take it all in.

His hand grips around his shaft, then he gently moves it up and down, inches away from my mouth.

A moan escapes me as I watch his pace move faster. The sounds he makes drive me crazy until his groan warns me he is just about to finish.

"Will you swallow?" he asks, out of breath.

I lick my lips, then gaze into his burning eyes. "Every last drop."

He leans forward, blowing inside my mouth as his body continues to jerk from coming. I've never done this, only being told it's either hit or miss. The texture is odd but sweet, and I find myself swallowing, not sure what to do from here.

Hunter is desperately trying to catch his breath while he runs his thumb against my lip as he had earlier in the night.

"Now, we're even," he says with a sneer. "I guess we both know what happens when you turn twenty..."

I slowly stand as he zips up his pants.

"Don't get so cocky. I never said I'd fuck you."

His lips curve upward into a smile. "I'd love to watch you try to resist."

TWENTY

"Happy birthday!"

April throws herself over me on the bed, forcing me to wake. Beneath her overbearing embrace, I'm squashed into the mattress, barely able to breathe.

"You're squashing me at some ungodly hour of the morning," I strain.

She slides off yet continues to lay on her side, propping her head up with her elbow resting on the bed.

"But it's your birthday. You're no longer a teen!"

I purposely let out a groan over April's high-pitched voice. It should be illegal to be this energized in the morning. Although, from memory, when April turned twenty a few months back, I also recall torturing her.

My eyes close unwillingly, exhausted from barely any sleep. I'd spent the night back and forth texting with Hunter. Since the 'incident' in the elevator, I haven't seen him. At least this time, he told me there were rescheduled meetings in Denver, so he flew out the next day.

Last night began with a simple how-was-your-week text

and ended with all the dirty things he plans to do to me. Hunter is an intelligent man. He knew what happened in the elevator left me sexually frustrated, and I needed a release last night.

Though, he made it clear I wasn't to come. Not without him watching. I don't know why I obeyed his stupid rule because it's left me in a not-so-pleasant mood this morning.

"Time to get out of bed. We have a big day planned."

"Do we have to?" I mumble into the pillow. "Sleep is a nice birthday present."

"If you don't get up, I'll make you wear the leg warmers," April threatens.

"Fine."

After showering, I change into this cute white skater-style dress. It's short, but given it's hot out, appropriate for the weather. Inside the closet, I decide on a pair of shoes. April hasn't given any context to our activities, so I opt for my white Nike Air Force 1's. With an all-white outfit, I pray she doesn't plan anything messy.

The heat forces me to tie my hair into a ponytail away from my face. Before I leave the room, I sit at the edge of my bed and read all my messages. Millie and Ava are already awake and the first to greet me happy birthday.

I tap into my DMs and see a message from Beau.

BROMANO

Happy birthday, princess. No longer a teen. How adult of you.

ME

Thanks... I'm not sad to leave my teenage years behind. Time to do all the fun things without judgment.

The bubble appears. Of course, he is awake, given it's after nine in New York.

> **BROMANO**
>
> Alexa Edwards have fun... is that even possible?

> **ME**
>
> You're supposed to be nice to me. It is my birthday, after all.

> **BROMANO**
>
> Okay, fine. You're so beautiful, and I hope you have the best day ever.

> **ME**
>
> That's more like it. See, it wasn't so bad to be a nice boy, now was it?

> **BROMANO**
>
> I need to show you I'm a man.

> **ME**
>
> The next time I visit Manhattan. Take me to some wrestling match or something.

> **BROMANO**
>
> That's not what I was thinking, Alexa.

I reread his last message, and maybe it's just me, but is he insinuating sex? Surely, it's me and my dirty mind right now. I've been conditioned to think men only want sex. Beau has never shown interest in me. If anything, we've never truly gotten along.

Unsure where to go from here, I think of something witty but decide to leave it for now.

April texts me to meet her in the kitchen. I grab my things and make my way there, trying to juggle responding to the messages now flooding my phone. Surprised to see a message from my dad, I quickly responded thank you.

Then, I glance up to see April, Hunter, and Kathy all at the table.

"Surprise," April cheers with a big smile on her face. "Your first official breakfast with my family."

Kathy stands up to hug me, followed by wishing me a happy birthday. As Hunter rises from his chair, I beg him not to touch me. His eyes dance in delight, almost as if he's picturing me naked on all fours because I'm officially twenty years old.

Great, now I'm picturing myself naked on all fours with him behind me.

I bite down on my lip as he extends his hand politely. "Happy birthday, Alexandra."

My hand rests in his, the simple touch sending a frenzy through me, but I pull away quickly as Kathy and April watch us.

"Thank you."

"Please, take a seat." He motions, pulling the chair out for me. "Our chef has prepared a wonderful breakfast to begin your celebrations."

The seat is beside April, and thankfully, she is the buffer between Hunter and me. As soon as I sit, the chef introduces himself as Gerald, then announces the menu. A server appears with coffee and juice before bringing out the food.

"Alexa, any big plans for your birthday?" Kathy asks while cutting her croissant. "Twenty is such an important time in your life."

"April apparently has plans for me," I mention, glancing at April. "Something exciting, no doubt."

"Only the best for my bestie." She grins, taking a bite of her omelet. "You know what would make this day even better?"

"What?" I smile, knowing whatever she says will be something ridiculous, like wearing leg warmers in the middle of summer. I take a sip of my coffee while waiting for April to tell me.

"Finding you a boyfriend."

The hot liquid catches in my throat, making me cough involuntarily. My eyes briefly gaze at Hunter, but his head is down, staring at his plate. Beside his glass of juice, his fist is clenched tight, angered by April's comment. I don't understand why. We're just fooling around, and there's nothing serious going on.

"April, leave Alexa alone," Kathy gently scolds. "Twenty is the age to be young and free. When I was twenty, you were starting school. Trust me, have fun and enjoy the freedom while you can."

"I don't mean get a boyfriend and get knocked up," April drags.

My gaze falls upon the plate of food in front of me. If I had Cole's baby, I would have a toddler right now to be responsible for. I highly doubt Cole and I would have lasted, so trying to co-parent with him would have been a nightmare.

Then, it dawns on me it's been a long time since I've thought about what happened between us. The nightmares have stopped, and life has just been so busy, which means I haven't had time to think.

And someone else has been occupying my mind.

Hunter is still quiet across the table, prompting April to continue the conversation.

"Look, we're all adults here. How about just a fling then?"

This is getting worse by the minute.

"April," Hunter clears his throat, but his expression is

stern. "Some things are best not discussed in an open forum."

April lets out a huff and rolls her eyes in boredom. "Fine, in that case, let's go, Alexa. What happens on your birthday apparently stays between us."

I place my napkin on the table, barely eating a bite of food. Politely, I say goodbye and only briefly look at Hunter. He's good at keeping his expression at bay, showing no emotion or anything to give away what we've done.

"Have fun, girls," Kathy says before turning to Hunter to discuss another event.

As we leave the room, I pull April aside. "You could have warned me he would be at breakfast. Do you know how awkward it is staying in your boss's house?"

"Relax... Hunter is pretty chilled. Although lately, he has been a bit crabby. Probably got his man period or something."

We head outside, where a pink mustang is parked with a man sitting in the driver's seat.

"What is this?" I laugh, noting the car looks like it belongs to Barbie.

"Ta-da!" She raises her arm in the air. "Our ride for the day so we can enjoy all the festivities and drink."

"Drink? You do know I'm still only twenty?"

"Eh." She shrugs. "A little drinking hurt no one."

We hop into the car, placing our seat belts on, then I quickly check my phone. A text from Hunter came through two minutes ago.

HUNTER

Enjoy your birthday, but tonight, you're all mine.

"Why the face?" April questions, furrowing her brows. "Dirty birthday text? Show me!"

I quickly hit delete, panicked she'll read it. "Nothing like that, just my cousin."

When April said drinking hurt no one, boy was she wrong. Since we legally couldn't buy any alcohol, she made sure the car had a cooler full of it.

Our first stop is rollerblading in Venice Beach, but really April just wants to stop at Muscle Beach Gym and drool over the men working out. There is a lot of sweat and grunting, both of which I find very unappealing.

Next, the driver takes us to this cute little book café the next beach down. The space is so quaint with bookshelves everywhere you look, housing classics to some more recent works.

April organized a little tea party, but we are so buzzed we just can't stop laughing long enough to eat. We manage to eat some food until the waiter comes out with a cupcake and a burning candle.

"Aww, you didn't have to." The entire café sings happy birthday, then April offers cupcakes to everyone. "April, you can't afford this."

"It's your birthday, don't worry about that."

Our next stop is bowling, which is so much more fun when drunk, followed by our last stop of the day—the tattoo parlor.

"God, my dad will kill me," I mutter, looking at the wall of designs.

"Get it some place he won't see."

April picks out the bunny ears since she's obsessed with rabbits. It's such a bizarre tattoo, but she doesn't care, sitting in the chair so they can ink her ankle.

As I continue to glance at the wall, nothing catches my

attention until I stumble on an anchor with wild roses wrapping around it. It's perfect.

The other tattoo artist directs me to lie down, covering my bottom half with a sheet as I pull my dress up to ink it just below my panty line. It'll be inked just above my public bone so it can be hidden when I wear bikini bottoms.

It doesn't take long, even when we lie and say we haven't had a single thing to drink. The pain isn't too bad, more annoying than painful.

When we both finish, April pays for our tattoos, much to my disappointment.

"April, you've done enough already. Why did you pay for me?"

"It's your birthday, silly."

"You shouldn't have spent so much money on me today."

April purses her lips, staring at me oddly, then releases a breath. "Hunter gave me his credit card. He kind of said it was on him."

"But... but..." I stammer, unable to process my thoughts. "Why would he do that?"

"Because he can. He has more money than he knows what to do with," April assures me. "Look, don't tell him I told you, okay?"

I nod, but I can only think about how I just branded myself, and he paid for it.

Something I'm now forced to remember forever.

―――――

"Happy birthday to you!"

Eric's voice is the loudest over everyone's, maybe because he drank too much Japanese sake. There was an egging incident. The chef told him 'catch,' Eric got cocky, then splat all over his Balenciaga shirt.

We all laughed way too hard while Eric actually cried. Mom then ordered the sake and got him drunk. It was much easier this way to tolerate him.

It was an enjoyable night with my sisters and their husbands, though Addy and Masen weren't able to make it. Ava has it in her head that Addy is pregnant, but that's just Ava being Ava. She thinks *everyone* is pregnant.

My father is sitting beside Mom, and for the most part, he's not acting like a dick for once and enjoying himself.

It kind of makes for a perfect end to the night, at least, if this is how the night ends.

I check my phone to see the time. It's almost ten-thirty, plus no text from Hunter. April parted ways with me just after six, and I came straight here. Maybe Hunter is all talk. He is just teasing me because he can.

Men are such assholes.

"I heard you've found yourself a job," Dad mentions cautiously before we end the night. "Are you enjoying it?"

"Uh, yeah," I respond while scratching the back of my neck. "Hunt, I mean Mr. Cash, is nice enough."

Dad cocks his head, pausing to examine me. It's been a long while since I've been under the Lex Edwards' microscope. *God, does he know I'm fooling around with my older boss?*

"I heard you reported to Cash's assistant, not him?"

"I was, but things got busy. The company has been busy acquiring other companies, so I was asked to take on more work."

"I'm well aware of the acquisitions," he informs me with a confident stance. "And have you thought more about how a college education can help further your career?"

"Dad," I murmur, lowering my eyes. "I don't want to fight with you tonight."

"I don't want that either, Alexa."

Suddenly, the karaoke machine comes on, and Eric climbs onto the stool, belting out his rendition of "It's Raining Men." I'm not fond of old music, but this song is always fun to sing along to.

I check my phone again to see the time.

"Got somewhere you need to be?" Millie probes, crossing her arms with a knowing grin. "You know, when midnight strikes, it's just another day."

"Nowhere," I answer with disappointment. "There's been no text or anything for plans. I'm happy to stay here and watch Eric make a fool out of himself."

It doesn't last long since the restaurant kicks us out at eleven thirty. We all say goodbye to each other, but I realize I don't have a ride home.

"We'll take you," Millie offers as Will pulls up in his car.

I hug everyone again but stop just shy of my father. He had one drink, at best, since he has to drive, so I know he's thinking rationally, and whatever he is just about to say will probably be exactly what he has been thinking.

"Good luck with everything, Alexa."

"Um, thanks, Dad."

On the car ride home, I lean forward between Will and Millie.

"Don't you think it was weird how Dad was just like... good luck, Alexa?"

Millie draws in a breath. "That's what you wanted."

"Yes, but it was weird. He did question me working for Hunter and not Meredith."

"You call him Hunter?" Will asks out of nowhere.

Millie immediately glares at him. I glance at her, then at

Will. I bet she said something! How hard is it to keep a conversation between two sisters?

"I told you not to say anything!"

"I never breathed a word to Ava. Will is my husband. There are certain rules surrounding marriage."

"Like what?" I question in annoyance.

"You tell each other everything," she states.

My mouth sets into a hard line as I find this hard to believe. "Everything?"

"Yes, and it stays between us."

I turn to look at Will again. "Is this true?"

He simply nods. "I didn't make up the rules. So, you call your boss by his first name?"

"And?"

"Nothing," he vaguely replies. "However, you're reporting to him now?"

My jaw and neck become tight as I tug on the seat belt to loosen it. "He's married. Even you know that."

"Right," Will muses. "His marriage of convenience which means he's not in love. Then in walks this young girl who happens to be the daughter of Lex Edwards."

I jerk forward, placing my hands on their seats for support.

"What are you trying to say?"

"Will, stop," Millie demands, raising her voice. "Don't go off on your tangent..."

His lips pinch together in frustration. "Amelia, I love you, but you don't understand a guy's perspective. Just like I don't understand a woman's."

"Okay, fine," I tell them both. "Give me your guy's perspective."

"Men in power do, or should I say manipulate, certain

situations to get what they want. You reporting to Hunter means you work closely with only him, am I correct?"

"Yeah..."

"And does it mean you're often alone together?"

"I wouldn't say often," I mumble.

"So, Hunter Cash wants the trophy of Lex Edwards' daughter," Will so blatantly informs me.

"It's not like that."

He tilts his head, keeping his eyes fixated on the road. "Oh, so what is it like when you're alone, and he whispers dirty things to you? Please don't tell me you're falling in love with him."

"Will!" Millie throws her head back, angry at him. "Give her a break. In case you haven't noticed, you weren't exactly innocent when we first got together."

"Yeah." He smirks, remaining quiet for a moment. "That's how I know, Amelia."

I sit back again in the seat to think about what Will said. Things are different with Hunter and me. Aside from the night he drove me home, he has never mentioned my father. If I was a so-called trophy, surely he would have talked or said something to allude to this.

The house appears out of nowhere, my thoughts consuming me for the rest of the drive. After I punch in the code for the gate and Will pulls up, he turns in his seat to face me.

"Be careful, Alexa," he warns, then sighs. "Our home is yours to stay in whenever you need it. Don't feel like you have to live here to prove a point to Lex, okay?"

I barely manage the nod, simply smiling while opening the door.

Amelia gazes at me with sympathy. "I'll call you tomorrow, okay?"

Without another word, I exit the car and watch it drive off. As if I'm on autopilot, I open the main doors to darkness once again. Glancing at the roof, I wait for the lights to sense me and turn on, but they don't.

Drawing my brows in confusion, my eyes immediately gaze upon Hunter standing at the foot of the large staircase in the dark.

"I've been waiting for you," he says in a seductive tone.

"But, you never text—"

He walks toward me, keys jingling in his hand. Suddenly, he grabs my hand, gripping it tight.

"Let's go," he demands.

I'm walking fast to keep up with him. "Where are we going?"

Stopping midstep, he turns to face me, cupping my chin in his hand. My breathing grows faster and more audible until he leans down and places his lips on mine.

"To do what we've both been waiting for," Hunter murmurs. "But not here. My penthouse because I need you naked all night long."

TWENTY-ONE

HUNTER

Alexandra Edwards.

How the name ignites a fire within me, one I haven't been able to control since the moment April asked for her to stay at the house.

You'd be a fool not to know who Lex Edwards is, and despite me knowing everything about the mogul, I'd not made an effort to learn anything about his family.

Of course, I knew he was married and had daughters. I only knew the oldest was married to Will Romano, but that was it. When it comes to family, I don't really give a shit. I barely had any of my own, and the ones who did call themselves family only wanted one thing from me.

Money.

That's all people have wanted from me my whole life. My parents were killed in a car accident when I was five, leaving me to be raised by my grandfather. He was the patriarch of the family, and everyone knew he would leave his fortune to his only grandchild.

With a condition, of course.

He didn't want me to be lonely, like him, so the condition was to marry someone, and the family's estate and hold-ings were mine.

I was given no choice.

Not when hungry thieves were waiting to get their hands on it.

Marrying Kathy was easy, she wanted money, and I had plenty of it. At the time, it didn't bother me she had a daughter. We had an agreement: she could live in the house and do whatever the hell she wanted, and I'll keep my pent-house to live in. If the situation called for it, to keep up appearances, I did have a room in the house.

Our marriage is one of pure convenience. With an unlimited Amex, Kathy has no interest in what I do with my life, just like I have no interest in hers. Spend all the money you want, just leave me the fuck alone.

It was all working fine until Alexandra Edwards came to stay.

I'd barely been staying at the house, but curiosity got the better of me, and one night I saw her come back home. Not wanting to introduce myself, I stayed behind the pillar inside the foyer and watched her creep into her room.

It was dark, so I barely caught a glimpse of her, but then April begged me to hire her.

It was against my policy to hire someone just because they needed a job. However, if there was a role available, they were welcome to apply for it like everyone else.

Meredith needed her, and Alexandra needed to prove to her she was the best person for the job.

The moment I saw her in proper lighting in the office, I was surprised to see this beautiful woman. It made no sense why she would stay in my house and work at my company if her father was one of the wealthiest men in the world.

However, Lex Edwards is also a bully.

My fascination became an obsession, one I tried to control by distancing myself and traveling to avoid seeing her in the office. I knew getting involved or even touching Alexa could have dire consequences, but she was too hard to resist.

My guard crumbled the night of Hendricks' launch party in Malibu, and I succumbed to needing to find out more. It turned out that she had no interest in discussing whatever was going on with her father. What did it matter to me? All I knew was that business dealings were happening to push my company to the number one spot in media.

Dealings that will affect Lex Edwards.

Then, it all took a turn. I'd started imagining her beneath me, the soft skin I'd noticed on the car ride home and the perky tits teasing me in the pantry.

Alexandra has this innocence about her, but what shocked me was her kink to pleasure herself in front of me. Sure, I pushed her, but she never once hesitated.

***

I park the car in the garage beneath the building and quickly exit to open her door. As she steps out, I pin her against the car, desperate to taste her lips again. She tastes sweet, like candy, and something else I can't explain.

"Hunter," she moans in between our heated exchange. "Someone will see us here."

My hand glides down her stomach, then between her legs. I watch her expression, the way she bites her lips so teasingly. I'm going crazy waiting, needing to be inside her now.

"I don't care," I grit, but she grips my hand to stop me. "Alexandra..."

"I will let you touch me..." she agrees, trying to catch her breath, "... but just for a moment, then upstairs."

She moves my hand inside her panties, and I bite on my tongue, tasting blood when my fingers brush against her clit.

"Fuck."

Her hand reaches for my belt just to bring me in closer. My fingers glide so effortlessly, drenched in how wet she is for me right now.

"We need to go upstairs now," she commands.

Removing my hand, I hear a slight whimper, but refusing to waste any more time, we make our way to the elevator.

I don't hold back inside the elevator, pinning her against the mirror wall and ravaging her with kisses. When the door pings open, I quickly pull her along to the penthouse, desperate to get her naked in my bed.

I punch in the code to the door, stuffing it up because my brain is foggy.

"If I screw this up again, the alarms will go off, but I don't care. I'm fucking you right here."

Alexandra places her hand on mine in an effort to calm me down. "Think carefully. The next four digits will dictate how many times you'll be fucking me tonight."

Eight, five, one, eight.

Open.

I pull Alexandra in, no words left to be said as we walk toward my room. Inside, I bring her body in flush with mine but take a moment to stare into her eyes.

"Once we do this," I warn her in a low voice.

She nods quietly. "I know..."

Neither one of us says the words, but we both know there is no turning back. Everything will change.

How much, I have no clue.

As we stand by the bed, I lift her dress over her head, revealing her white lace panties and matching bra. Even in the dark, the lace is see-through, showing me her nipples. *Okay, control yourself.*

Never in my life have I had to practice such self-control, fighting the urge to just tear it all off and bend her over.

But Alexandra is different.

My hands move on their own accord, taping behind the back of her neck and then trailing down between her beautiful tits. As I continue to tease down her body, I see the bandage peeking out from the elastic of her panties.

"This explains the charge on my credit card." I smirk, circling around it. "Does it hurt?"

She shakes her head. "No, but it depends on how rough you are with me."

My mouth takes hers, our tongues battling in a frenzy. "I promise you're in good hands."

I stop all this fussing around, removing her garments so she's naked in my bed. She's so fucking beautiful, every curve, every inch of her. In a rush, I remove my own clothes, then carry her into the bed as I lay on top of her, careful not to rub against her bandage.

"Happy birthday," I say in a low voice. "You don't know how long I've been waiting for this."

Her prolonged stare does something to me, the emerald in her eyes making me want to own her completely, allowing no one to touch her, ever.

"How long?" she whispers.

"Long enough to ruin me."

A shallow sigh escapes her pink lips before she reaches

down and wraps her hand around my cock. The small strokes are almost enough to make me come, but I strain and hold back.

"No more waiting," she murmurs, guiding me with her hand until my shaft is suddenly warm and wet inside her. Fuck, she's tight.

We move in sync as I tug on her nipples, desperate to blow on every inch of her. I quickly stop when I can feel her tense beneath me, ready to come.

"On top," I demand. "I need to see you come for me."

Our bodies move in position, and when she's riding me so effortlessly, I watch her come all over my cock, then follow as my body explodes from the sensation ripping through me.

"*Fuck,*" I groan, gripping her hips.

We both try to catch our breath, but I'm far from done. Demanding she climb off, I spread her legs in front of me and devour the sight of her pussy in front of me.

I've been with a lot of women, but never have I seen a woman so beautiful waiting for me to eat her out like it's my last meal on Earth.

"Are you ready to come again?" I ask, blowing soft air on her clit.

Her head falls back into the pillow, but then, she grabs my hair and pushes my mouth onto her. I suck her clit gently, listening to her moans. When I hear her pace pick up and see her back arch, I slide two fingers inside and increase my speed.

My lips suck harder, but not for long. A long moan escapes her mouth as she clutches the pillows behind her, and again, I watch her come before me.

I'm still fucking hard, so I turn her over despite her exhaustion.

"On all fours, I need to fuck you again."

She doesn't argue, positioning her ass in front of me. *Oh, what I would give to be inside this tight ass hole of hers.*

Spreading her cheeks wide, I slide myself in, then breathe out to give myself a second to slow my body down. As I begin to move, my hands grip tight on her ass, but the temptation is too much. My thumb eases its way over her ass hole, slowly entering as she gasps and pushes back to me. She doesn't say no, so I continue pumping into her until my muscles tighten, and my whole body shudders as I explode in her.

"Jesus, fuck," I expel a string of profanities, unable to see straight.

It takes me moments to calm down enough so I can pull myself out. Alexandra collapses on the bed at the same time I do. With the bedsheet pulled over us, I bring her back to me and kiss her shoulder.

"Hunter, I'm on birth control," she mumbles, followed by a sigh. "We didn't talk about it."

I close my eyes, annoyed I didn't even stop to think. Fuck! What the hell is wrong with me? I don't want a family or pesky kids despite my grandfather pushing me before his death to have children.

"Fuck," I mouth again. "I'm sorry... I was—"

"It's okay," she reassures me. "I'm always on top of birth control since..."

She trails off, which piques my curiosity. "Since what?"

"Uh, just since high school."

It makes sense, unlike Kathy, who had April at some ridiculous age. It's smart to be safe.

My hand reaches around to cup her tits. As she continues to lay beside me, I listen to her soft breaths while we fall into a momentary silence.

"Stay," I tell her.

"Tonight?"

I turn her around, wanting to kiss her lips. "Yes, tonight. I'm not done."

A sly smile plays on her lips. "What else did you have in mind?"

"God," I mutter, biting my lip as I grow hard again. "Everything."

We spend the night in a constant state of euphoria. I fuck her endlessly, on all fours again, up and against the window. We shower together, careful to protect her tattoo with a waterproof bandage, but I can't help pushing her up against the wall and then making her get on her knees to suck me off.

As the sun rises, we stumble back to bed, and I see her slowly drift off to sleep.

"Alexandra," I whisper, careful not to startle her.

"Hmm..."

"We can't be seen together. You do understand that?"

"Uh-huh." She yawns. "You're married..."

I kiss her shoulder again, battling whether or not to tell her the truth. At least, I can tell her half the truth.

"My marriage to Kathy is not what you think."

Alexandra opens her eyes wide, suddenly awake. She props herself up on her elbows, staring at me in curiosity.

"What do you think I think?"

"I think you think we are ordinary husband and wife. We sleep in the same bed. We fuck each other."

"Okay... so you don't sleep in the same bed?"

"I don't touch her." I lower my voice, keeping my gaze fixated on hers. "I've never touched her."

"Let me get this straight. You've never fucked Kathy? Like ever?"

I shake my head. "Our marriage is of convenience."

Alexandra remains quiet, lost in thought. "We don't need to talk about it anymore, for now. You've said what I wanted to know."

My fingers reach to caress her bottom lip. "There's only one thing I want right now."

She laughs, slapping my chest. "I think I'm broken."

I grab the bed sheet and toss it over the side of the bed, allowing my cock to spring free.

"You may be broken," I say with an urge in my tone. "But I am most certainly not. Now, get on all fours and suck me off. Boss's orders."

TWENTY-TWO

ALEXA

Hunter did break me.

The man is insatiable.

We'd spent all of Sunday in bed, only leaving to eat. I struggled to walk, red and raw from the copious amount of sex we had. In my wildest dreams, I never experienced letting go of my inhibitions the way I did, but with Hunter, I felt this freedom to be myself.

It's kind of cute he felt sorry for me, drawing me a bath to soak in. It was a bit of a struggle since the water needed to be low to protect my still-fresh tattoo.

Of course, it started as a bath, then ended up with me on my knees as he demanded I give him a blow job.

I sit on the sofa as he turns the television on and searches for something interesting to watch. It gives me an opportunity to catch up on my messages. Ava, no surprise, is blowing up my phone.

"Argh," I complain out loud.

Hunter glances over. "What's wrong?"

"My sister, she's annoying, that's all."

He diverts his attention to the screen, settling on some finance channel.

"So, you have how many sisters?"

"Three." I sigh. "Amelia, but we call her Millie, is the oldest. She's a lawyer and married with three boys. Ava is next. She's the annoying one."

"There's always one, I guess."

"Ava is married to Austin, Millie's ex-fiancé. They have two daughters together."

Hunter cocks his head. "Your sister married your older sister's ex-fiancé?"

"Yeah, I know. I couldn't make this stuff up even if I tried."

"And your other sister?"

"Addison lives in San Francisco. She got married last year. No kids yet because she just finished her degree in Psych. Though, Ava seems to think there's something brewing. Her words, not mine."

With his arm resting behind me on the sofa, Hunter looks so casual and sexy in a pair of gray sweats and a white tee. Very different from the man I see inside the office.

"So, all your names start with the letter A?"

"Yeah," I drag with a forced smile. "My father's name is Alexander, so I guess my parents thought that would be fun."

Hunter nods but falls into a digestive silence. I'm not sure what to say, so I go back to responding to Ava to tell her I'm alive, just busy.

"I've actually met your father at a summit," Hunter admits with a blank expression. "Interesting man."

"Interesting?" I hold back laughing at the choice of words. "My father is not interesting."

"You seem to have a certain opinion of him."

"He's controlling, stubborn, and frankly, an asshole when he doesn't get his way."

The moment it leaves my mouth, I feel somewhat better that my opinion is out in the open. No more hiding how I feel about the man.

"And you've said all these things to him?" Hunter questions with a smirk.

"Yes," I admit, bowing my head. "It's why I went to Europe, met April, and applied for this job. We don't get along."

"But your sisters do?"

I begin to fidget with the cushion sitting on my lap. "They adore him. He treats them like they're queens."

Hunter purses his lips, then tilts his head. "I'm surprised you have the backbone to go up against Lex Edwards. Many have tried and failed. It explains why you had no problem speaking to me."

My elbow purposely knocks into his side, causing him to scowl.

"You're cute outside the office. Why do you act like a jerk when wearing the suit?"

"Alexandra, you know I'm still your boss, right?"

"Yeah, but you won't fire me. I've got something you want."

He rubs his chin as I climb on top of him, a grin spreading across his face. "What exactly is that?"

"You're just about to find out..."

———

It's one thing to be alone with Hunter in his penthouse, but another to be around him inside a bustling office.

I went back to the main house on Sunday night since

April had a crisis. Her tampon was stuck, and Kathy was out as usual. We were no longer period sisters, much to April's disappointment. Her cycle started arriving earlier.

I may not have many skills, but tampon removal happens to be one of them.

Hunter informed me his week is booked out with meetings, dinners, and a day trip to Silicon Valley. Naturally, I told him it's fine since we're not in a relationship. He has his life, and I have mine.

Although, I don't really have a life. Just a bestie I'm lying to, plus sisters who continue to blow up my phone with the latest gossip.

With Hunter in and out of the office, it makes work life easier. I manage to get a lot done, working closely with Meredith, who has been feeling unwell of late.

"Are you sure you don't want to go home?" I ask, examining how her shoulders slump as she occasionally clutches onto her chest. "You really should see a doctor."

"It's fine," she reassures me as I stare at her with concern. "I'll tell you what, if I don't feel well after lunch, then I'll go visit the doctor."

"Good."

I exit her office and run into Josh.

"Oh, hey," I greet, surprised to see him since it's been a while. "Sorry I haven't gotten back to you about hanging out. I've been super busy."

Josh flattens his lips but quickly forces a smile. "It's fine. Actually, today is my last day."

"Your last day? You're leaving."

"They're transferring my role to the Denver office. I agreed to go."

"I guess goodbye is in order."

I reach out to hug him, ignoring how stiff he is in my

embrace. When I pull back, Hunter enters his office with clients but continues to stare at me with a pinched expression.

"It was nice knowing you, Alexa," Josh says before walking back to his desk.

Lunchtime in the office is always deserted, except for the geeks who hang around eating homemade sandwiches while collecting coins on some stupid game on their phone.

Just as I'm about to grab something, Hunter calls me into his office. I quickly make my way over, then enter his office to find him alone.

"I was about to grab some lunch."

"Why were you hugging Josh?" he questions but doesn't look my way.

"Uh, because that's what you do when saying goodbye to a friend. You never mentioned he was leaving?"

"Not all work matters can be discussed, Alexandra. Some need to remain confidential."

"Fine," I snap. "Is that what you called me in for? To get jealous over some guy I've never had sex with?"

Hunter lifts his gaze in line with mine but follows with sighing dejectedly. "I'm sorry, and that's not why I called you in. I wanted to take you out to lunch."

The door is still open, so I keep my voice low. "Do you think it's a good idea?"

"I take Meredith out all the time."

"Well then..." I muse, "... lunch it is."

There is no opportunity to do or say anything inappropriate. The elevator was full to the lobby. The sidewalk was bustling with people. Hunter chose a restaurant a block from the office, but it was also busy, with almost every seat taken.

We ordered quickly, which resulted in the food arriving

nice and hot. Our conversations mainly centered around work and all the things Hunter needed me to do.

"You know, I can't stay your assistant forever."

Hunter parts his lips slightly. "Why not?"

"It's not my forever job."

"What is your forever job?"

"I don't know yet," I answer openly. "When I was a kid, I wanted to be a doctor."

The moment it comes out, something stirs inside of me. I still remember the night of the party when the guy almost drowned and how saving his life was something I'd never experienced before.

"You need to go to college for that."

"I'm well aware of that."

"Then, tell me. Why didn't you go to college? From what you've told me about your sisters, all of them have quite impressive careers."

"It wasn't right for me at the time."

He finishes the remains of his drink, waiting for me to respond. "And now?"

"I haven't thought about it much," I admit, wiping the corner of my mouth with the napkin. "I've been occupied, in case you haven't noticed."

"Oh..." Hunter grins with dancing eyes. "I've noticed, but if we're being honest here, it's been three whole days since I've been inside you."

My eyes widen in disbelief. Did he just say that out loud? Anyone could have heard. My cheeks flush as the temperature inside the restaurant rises.

"What if someone heard you?" I whisper.

Hunter removes his credit card, handing it to the server, who takes it, then returns with it soon after.

"Shall we leave in case anyone hears about all the things I'm going to do to you tonight?" he teases.

I hold back from slapping his arm and instead exit the restaurant with the right mind to give him a good blasting once no one can listen. Just as I'm about to open my mouth, my eyes fall upon a familiar face walking toward me.

"Cole," I whisper in shock.

He recognizes me immediately, a genuine smile adorning the once handsome face I would kiss daily. Suddenly, my eyes move toward his chest to see a baby carrier.

"Alexa?"

I offer my best smile, still surprised to see him. Cole looks different, more mature.

"Cole, oh my god, it's been—"

"A long time," he finishes.

"You have a baby," I point out, swallowing the lump inside my throat from seeing him as a daddy.

"Her name is Charlotte," he announces proudly. "I know, just like your mom. It's always been Madaline's favorite name, so..."

"Of course." I lean over to better observe the baby. She has tiny features but is cute and sleepy. "She's beautiful, Cole. Congratulations."

Hunter clears his throat beside me, waiting with an impatient stare.

"Oh, sorry. Cole, this is my boss, Hunter Cash."

Cole extends his hand. "Nice to meet you."

"And you," Hunter responds in a bored tone.

"Cole and I went to high school together."

Hunter nods, pressing his lips flat.

"Listen, congrats again on the baby." My stomach

churns, bringing on a queasy feeling. "Good luck with everything."

"You too." He smiles while stroking Charlotte's hair. "Oh, say hi to Ava. She's stopped pestering me via text. I hate to admit I miss it."

I manage to laugh. "Lucky for you."

As I wave goodbye, I walk quietly alongside Hunter with a heavy heart. Seeing Cole with his new baby evoked so many buried emotions. I can dissect it all I want, but the truth is, it hurts like fucking hell. It could have been our baby.

"Is everything okay?" Hunter questions.

"Yeah."

"So, did you guys date or something?"

I nod. "For most of the senior year."

Hunter doesn't say another word but is soon distracted as his phone rings. He takes the call, so I opt to give him privacy, walking a few steps ahead of him.

For the rest of the afternoon, I'm unable to concentrate. My pen doodles circles on my notepad as I'm lost in thought. I keep replaying Cole's face in my head, how he looks so happy and content. How I assumed he wouldn't want a child and football would have been more important.

My phone pings as Hunter summons me to his office. I walk over slowly, knocking on the door as usual, then enter upon him saying, come in.

"So, I was thinking," he begins with, then continues, "Meredith isn't feeling well and usually accompanies me to New York. I'd like for you to join me."

"Me?" I point to my chest. "In New York?"

"Yes, for three days. Unless, of course, you have other plans?"

I shake my head. "This is work, though, right?"

"Yes, Alexandra. There is a gala event to which it will be good for you to get exposure."

"Okay, so when do we leave?"

"Tomorrow," he simply states.

"But... but..." I stammer, my head spinning with all the things I need to do. "I have to go home and pack."

"Go home and pack."

"You said—"

"Just tell April you're staying at your sister's house again, then drive over."

I hate lying to April. For the last week, I did my best to avoid her. It's not like she'd put two and two together. It's more the guilt eats away at me. Yesterday, I nearly ran into Kathy in the foyer. I made a sharp turn to avoid seeing her, panicked I would accidentally blurt out, 'I'm fucking your fake husband.'

"I guess I'll see you soon."

My back turns to exit the room until Hunter calls my name.

"Yes?"

"Is everything okay?"

I curve my lips upward and force a smile. "Perfectly fine."

TWENTY-THREE

It's been a long time since I'd set foot in Manhattan. As a child, we were here for a good part of the year. My parents still owned the same penthouse, and according to Ava, our rooms were exactly the same as when we were kids.

It's only supposed to be three days, but upon reviewing the schedule, Hunter only needed me for the gala event. His days were occupied with meetings I didn't need to attend.

To make sure no one accidentally saw us or the accounting team pick up on only one hotel charge, Hunter booked two hotel rooms, although he insisted I sleep with him.

As soon as we arrived, the change in time zone and flight caught up with me. I was exhausted and wanted to crash so hard, but Hunter had needs and made sure he fulfilled them even though sleep was the only thing I could think about.

When I woke the next day, he was gone. He briefly sent me a text to say he wouldn't be back until late. I told him I'd be working from the hotel room for a bit, then planned to catch up with my Uncle Rocky for lunch.

"Look at you, all beautiful and grown up." Uncle Rocky grins proudly. "No wonder Lex has turned gray."

"Salt and pepper is the correct term."

"Oh, yeah. Eric mentioned it once." He rolls his eyes, then blows a puff of air from his mouth in annoyance. "I'm not even going to tell you what he said afterward."

I cringe, knowing Eric is anything but vanilla with his opinions and views on life and men.

Uncle Rocky insists we have lunch near his work which happens to be in the Yankees Stadium since he is a sports commentator. I don't mind traveling to the Bronx, given I'd answered all my pending emails and nothing was urgent.

"This new job of yours, you like it?"

We sit at the small table in the back of the deli, both of us ordering Rueben sandwiches. Hunter enjoyed fancy restaurants, much like my father, but sometimes these small delis hit the spot with their food.

"I do. It was challenging at first, but I guess lately, it's gotten a lot easier."

"Oh yeah? You working for Cash, right?"

I nod, biting into my sandwich. It tastes so good, I accidentally let out a small moan.

Uncle Rocky lets out a whistle. "He and your father don't exactly get along."

"They don't? I thought they'd only met once. That's what Hunt, I mean Mr. Cash told me."

"I guess anyone can extend the truth."

"What do you mean?"

"Business is business, sweetheart. Men can get all macho about it," Uncle Rocky informs me. "They will protect their name and brand at all costs."

"I know that. I am Lex Edwards' daughter," I remind him.

"Exactly. Just be careful."

"Of what, exactly?"

Uncle Rocky watches me with a weighted gaze, but then he smiles and starts to talk about the sandwich. I'm glad we stopped talking about Hunter and Dad since I don't want to get caught in either one of their egotistical dramas.

After lunch, Uncle Rocky takes me back to the stadium for a tour. The tour involves the men's locker room which, to be honest, caught me by surprise.

"Eric would love this." I chuckle softly.

Uncle Rocky groans. "Trust me. He's been here. He claimed he had to discuss something with me, then all of a sudden, he's not in my office and supposedly lost his way... to the locker room."

"Thats so Eric." I laugh.

The stadium is huge, not that I'm a sports fan or anything, and I barely go to games of any sort. As Uncle Rocky continues his tour, his phone buzzes with a text, prompting him to read it.

"Ah, shit," he mumbles.

"What's wrong?"

"I'm supposed to drop off keys to Beau. We changed the locks on our place in the Hamptons, and he's going there tomorrow. The problem is, I've got two meetings this afternoon and a flight out to Cincinnati tonight."

"Oh, bummer."

"Hold on." Uncle Rocky motions for me to follow him back to his office. "Do you think you can drop them off when you head back to your hotel?"

"Uh, sure. Where exactly?"

"Beau lives on campus at NYU. I'll give you directions to get there."

It's not like I can say no since he seems to be in a bind. He scribbles something on a post-it note, then passes it to me along with the keys. It's the address and dorm room number.

A colleague of Uncle Rocky barges into his office with some major crisis, calling for Uncle Rocky's attention. I say goodbye quickly, then leave to catch a cab to NYU.

As I stand in the NYU courtyard, I can't help but admire the green trees surrounding the tall buildings. Students are sitting around, some in groups and a few by themselves. There's a lot of laughter from a group sitting near a tree, yet it doesn't seem to bother the students reading near them.

A warm feeling fills my chest, and I can't help but smile at all these people in their element. People who happen to be my age. It reminds me so much of high school, but with fewer cliques and judging by what everyone is wearing, everyone is just chilled doing their own thing.

I look down at my dress pants and blouse, not even remembering the last time I wore jeans and sneakers. Every day is corporate wear, which, to be brutally honest, is boring as fuck.

A part of me feels nostalgic like I'll never experience this. I take a breath, ignoring these thoughts because what's the point of dwelling on it?

Glancing down at the piece of paper, it's obvious my sense of direction is awful.

"Excuse me," I ask a girl walking past. "Do you know where this building is?"

She quickly reads the paper. "Sure, over there on your left."

"Thanks." I smile.

Making my way to where she pointed, I find the entrance without too much trouble. Beau's room is down the corridor as I track the numbers on the door. When I get closer, a guy stops me.

"You looking for someone?"

"Yeah." I hold up the paper, then point past him. "Just down there?"

A smirk graces his lips. "On the left. I'm Beau's room-mate, Kellan. And you are?"

"Alexa."

"Oh, Alexa Edwards?"

My brows draw in as I tilt my head with curiosity. "How do you know?"

"Beau's mentioned you. The name just stuck."

"Right..."

"Anyway, just go on in. The door is unlocked. He won't hear you knock. Usually, AirPods are in."

"Of course, it's all about studying."

Kellan grins. "Yeah... sure."

I thank Kellan, then continue down the corridor. It dawns on me I don't even know what Beau is majoring in because he's never mentioned anything that has to do with college. I'm surprised he even goes, to be honest.

The door is just on my left. As I place my hand to turn the knob, I realize I really should knock first but then hear music. He probably won't hear me. My hand twists the knob to open the door wide when my eyes fall upon Beau standing in the middle of the room as a girl is on her knees, sucking him off.

"Oh my god!" Beau lifts his head to meet my shocked gaze, but I clutch my chest in a state of panic. "I'm... I'm so sorry."

Panicked, I turn around in a mad rush and slam my face and arm against the edge of the door way. The pain ricochets in my mouth, causing me to see stars.

"Ouch," I cry.

"Alexa?" he calls in a raised voice. "Fuck, are you okay?"

I shake my head, but it hurts, and then I taste something weird on my lip.

"Brittany, get me an ice pack," Beau commands.

Even in my state of pain, I glance down to make sure he isn't naked below. Thankfully, his jeans are zipped up.

Brittany crosses her arms beneath her chest. "Who is she?"

"Never the fuck you mind," Beau shouts. "Just get me the goddamn ice pack."

"Get it yourself!" Brittany storms out of the room, staring me down like I'm some villain. If anything, I'm the victim here.

Beau retrieves the ice pack and demands I sit on his bed. Carefully, he places it on the corner of my lip as I gasp from the cold.

"What are you doing here?"

"Your dad asked me to drop the keys off."

"Oh," he mumbles.

"Yeah, oh, for me," I drag. "Your roommate told me I didn't need to knock."

Beau's nostrils flare in anger. "Kellan is a dick."

"He certainly is," I agree. "Look, I'm sorry I interrupted your activities."

As Beau continues to hold the ice pack to my lip, he doesn't say anything but continues to examine the cut near the corner of my mouth.

"I'm not sure how your lip got cut, and your nose survived."

"Big lips," I blurt out, then close my eyes in embarrassment. "Ignore that, please."

Beau chuckles. "Okay, sure. So, you never mentioned you were in the city."

"Last minute work thing."

"Work." He lingers with a smirk. "I forgot you sold out to the corporate life."

"Kind of had no choice," I admit, then sigh. "NYU is beautiful. I've never visited this campus. My cousin Andy went here."

"You missed out on the whole touring college campuses experience. Though, for me, it just made sense to stay in the city."

"What exactly do you want to major in?"

Beau shrugs his shoulders. "Not sure. I knew I needed to complete my undergraduate, and I guess we'll see what happens.

"So, you applied without a plan?"

He removes the ice pack to examine me again, moving closer so we're only inches apart.

"Too much pressure to decide at a young age. I'm sure I'll figure it out in the next few years."

It never occurred to me to attend college without direction. All my sisters knew exactly what they wanted to do. So did Mom and Dad. I'd been conditioned my whole life to think I had to know in senior year.

"Your lip looks bad," he murmurs, continuing to stare. "People will think I beat you up or something."

I place my hand on his shoulder jokingly. "You did beat me up, my brain, that is. I'm not sure if I can unsee what I saw."

Beau rubs the back of his neck. "Sorry, Brittany is just—"

"A girl who likes to give you blow jobs?"

"Yes, but we're not dating. It's all just casual."

"College life." I grin, then attempt to stand up, but my head spins. "Whoa. Did the ground move?"

Beau catches me as I stumble into his arms. "Okay, you need to lie down."

"I can't. I need to go back to the hotel."

"Alexa," he warns, bringing me down to his bed. "You need to rest, even just for an hour."

"Okay, I can manage an hour."

It doesn't take me long to doze off, given Beau's bed is soft and his sheets have this nice smell. When I wake, I let out a groan and wet my dry lips. Everything hurts, making it all the more difficult to sit up in bed.

"What time is it?" I croak, noticing the daylight has disappeared from the room.

Beau is sitting at his desk on his laptop with what appears to be some essay on the screen.

"It's seven," he informs me. "You slept for like four hours."

Panicked, I sit up in a rush. *"Four hours?"*

My head really hurts, and so does my lip. I reach into my purse to grab my phone.

Twenty missed calls.

Fifteen voicemails.

And ten text messages.

With my heart beating like a drum, I close my eyes momentarily and then open them to read the last text.

HUNTER

Where the fuck are you???

"I have to go," I rush, trying to balance myself upon standing up. "My boss is angry."

Beau grabs my arm to help me, and despite my reluctance, his support helps me focus better to avoid collapsing.

"Tell him you had an accident and you stayed here. What's the big deal?"

"I can't tell him I've fallen asleep in another guy's bed," I mumble.

Beau stares at me with tight eyes. "Why not?"

"It's unprofessional," I lie.

"You're fucking him," Beau insinuates in almost a growl. "Is that it?"

"Beau... stop."

"Does Lex know?"

I cross my arms with a pinched mouth. "What kind of a question is that?"

"It's a very valid question, Alexa." He paces the room, angered by the whole thing, which makes no sense. "It's like you purposely go out of your way to hurt your family!"

"Excuse me?" I bellow. "I do not do that!"

"Yeah, then give me one good reason you're fucking your boss. Of all the men you could have chosen, why him?"

I walk toward the door, opening it, but stop midstep. "What I do is none of your business. As for my family, you have no idea."

"That's where you're wrong, Alexa. When it comes to your family, I've known them my whole life. Lex is like a father to me. He doesn't deserve what you put him through. You need to wake up and realize your boyfriend will never replace the love of your father."

My eyes are blazing as my muscles quiver. "Go to hell, Beau Romano. You know nothing about me."

TWENTY-FOUR

HUNTER

"Are you listening, Mr. Cash?"

The voice over the phone fades out as I stand here staring out the window. From the thirty-second floor, the view is spectacular. I've always been fond of the city, never minding the hustle and bustle of the streets, but times call for a change.

This change is supposed to be a big one—new offices on the East Coast with expansion to the Caribbean in the next twelve months.

All these changes require substantial capital, something I assumed wouldn't be a problem until Joseph Albright, my grandfather's attorney, called to remind me of my side of the agreement.

"Hunter." Joseph uses my name this time, breaking my thoughts. "I've already gone out of my way to overturn your grandfather's will regarding the childbearing clause. The money was not to be released until you were married, with, or expecting a child. You assured me this would happen no later than twenty-four months after your nuptials. Time is running out, son."

I pinch the bridge of my nose to release the tension, but it doesn't work. Closing my eyes, the hostility runs deep. This life was thrust upon me. My grandfather wanted our family name to live on, and I'm the puppet in his master's show.

He's buried in the ground, yet he still controls my life.

Just let it all go. Money isn't everything.

The memory of him is so engrained it's become my living nightmare. I remember his dying wish as I held his hand on the hospital bed before he took his last breaths. His skin had turned gray, and the bone structure of his face was prominent. He barely had the strength to raise his hand to touch mine. In and out of consciousness, then his life ended right before my eyes.

The machines flatlined, the doctor called time of death, and then it was all over.

I wasn't given the opportunity to grieve the man who raised me when social services were about to take me away to live with a younger family. My grandfather stepped in, despite losing his wife, my grandmother, a year earlier to cancer.

Not one moment to grieve because everyone had their eye on the prize.

The family's fortune.

I just didn't understand why he insisted on having me marry and have children for the sake of the family's inheritance. This would have been a hell of a lot easier if he just gave it to me and trusted I would carry on the legacy.

But no, the last few weeks when he was incredibly ill, all he would talk about was loneliness and family meaning everything. As time began to run out, he changed his will only weeks before his death.

Joseph clears his throat over the phone. "Is there anything you'd like to add to this?"

"I need more time," I scorn.

"Well, you have a wife. Is it so bad to have a child? You might surprise yourself. Family is a blessing."

I can't think of anything worse than having a child with a woman I don't care about. If I loved her, perhaps things would be different. All of this is wrong and unethical, leaving me in a foul mood. I was supposed to come up with a plan to get out of this. At least, I hoped Joseph would just drop it.

"Are we done?"

"For now," Joseph informs me. "I'll be in touch soon. Mr. Cash, if you don't have a child, I'm afraid all the money will go back to the estate and be divided amongst the caretakers as per your grandfather's wish should you not fulfill his conditions."

I end the call without another word. The pain in my head only intensifies as my chest tightens. How the fuck am I supposed to get out of this? I refuse to ask Kathy to participate. We haven't even had sex. I made it clear when I proposed this arrangement I didn't want anything to convolute our platonic relationship.

She's not even the one you're thinking about.

Don't go there, I beg of myself.

There is one more meeting I need to attend, but my head is far from being switched on. As numbers were presented, I lost my patience, raising my voice and taking out my anger on whoever dared to challenge me. I knew it was out of character, but I couldn't shake this feeling of my whole life being controlled. It felt like I was trapped in some dungeon and handcuffed to the wall.

Then, Chester Jones brought up his plan to bring part

of Lex Edwards' company down. At least the part we were competing with. If we execute this right, Lex will lose a hell of a lot of money and stakeholder' confidence—two crucial things needed when dominating the business world.

"Lex Edwards will have no idea what's hit him," Chester reveals, leaning back in his chair with a smug expression. He's loathed Lex for as long as I've known him.

Alexandra's innocent green eyes flood my thoughts. I turn away from the screen, staring at the window again. No matter what I do, she's going to get hurt. It's not like I'm in love with her or anything, fuck, we aren't even dating or exclusive.

All I know is—no other man is allowed to touch her.

It's only me.

When I think about any man going near her, the adrenalin shoots through me, and all I want to do is kill whoever places his hands on her. Hell, sometimes it's even the intent. It's why I gave Josh the ultimatum. I didn't like him being friends with her or how naïve she was around him.

The jealousy is something I've never experienced. I dated girls in college, but they were just to pass the time. If I look back on the last ten years, I've never been in a serious or committed relationship. When I needed a quick fuck, I found it. End of story.

The meeting ends with me snapping at Chester, much to his surprise. The guy is smart, has some great ideas, but he's also a fucking sleaze at times. Meredith warned me to be careful, he may bring a strong clientele with him, but a sexual harassment case is the last thing our company needs.

I head back to the hotel, hoping Alexandra is done with her work so I can have her naked all night. Right now, I desperately needed to inhale the scent of her skin, the only thing consuming me of late.

She's become an obsession, one I'm struggling to break free from.

Back at the hotel, she's nowhere to be found. I checked her room, but it was empty. I tried to text her, then called her, and texted her again, but nothing. The last time she checked her email was hours ago.

Where the fuck is she?

It's unlike her not to answer anything. The sunlight begins to disappear as night falls over the city. I quickly pour myself a whisky, downing it in one go. Then, pour another as I pace the room, wondering how long I have to wait until I call 9-1-1.

If anything happens to her, I don't know what I'll do with myself. *Fuck, calm down.*

The beep of the swipe card causes me to dart my gaze onto the door. She enters the room with her head bowed, quietly closing the door behind her.

"Where the hell were you?" I question, raising my voice.

Slowly, she glances up, and the first thing I see is a cut on her lip. I rush over to her, panicked, examining the rest of her. "Alexandra, talk to me. What happened?"

"It's stupid," she begins in a low voice. "My uncle asked me to drop keys off to his son at NYU. I opened the door and kinda, well, never mind. Anyway, I ran into the door frame on my way out."

I take a step back, crossing my arms beneath my chest, the worry now turning into anger.

"Why didn't you answer your phone?"

Alexandra places her purse down on the bed and then folds her arms, keeping her distance from me.

"I fell asleep."

"You fell asleep?" I repeat, gritting my teeth. "Where exactly did you fall asleep?"

"On Beau's bed," she rushes, shaking her head. "It's not what you think. I was in so much pain when I hit the door, I felt so dizzy, so I sat down. It was worse when I tried to get up, so Beau suggested I lie down. It wasn't a concussion or anything, just pain and maybe the time difference that made me fall asleep. Look, I know it sounds weird, but it's the truth. Why would I lie?"

A slight growl expels from my lips as my fist clenches, resting beside my leg. A burning sensation spreads across my chest while I try to process what she just told me. She fell asleep in some college kid's bed and didn't have the decency to call or respond to the numerous text messages I sent.

As if I mean *nothing*.

"Exactly what did you see inside the room which made you turn around so fast you crashed into the door."

"Beau, being Beau." She tries to laugh it off. "A girl was pleasuring him."

The anger seeps through my veins. So, she saw him getting off with another girl and then fell asleep in his bed? My teeth clench as my jaw writhes in pain.

"Am I supposed to believe you just fell asleep in another guy's bed?" I question with a raised voice. "I was worried about you!"

"I'm sorry," she shouts in return. "God, I didn't sleep with him. Don't you trust me? Not that it would matter since we never agreed to be exclusive. How is that even possible when you're fucking married!"

"Alexandra," I warn, averting my gaze.

"No. Don't Alexandra me. You can think whatever the hell you want to think," she argues with blazing eyes. "I don't have to answer you. You don't own me. No one owns me. You are not my boyfriend."

She grabs her purse in a huff.

"Where the hell do you think you're going?"

Her lips press together thoughtfully. "Anywhere but here."

The door slams behind her, and just like a knife through the heart, reality has shown me the truth.

I've fallen in love with her.

And none of it matters because in less than six months, someone needs to be pregnant with my baby.

Or else I'm left with *nothing*.

TWENTY-FIVE

ALEXA

My hand taps on the door with a heavy sigh following.

It opens wide, and Beau stands in front of me with a surprised expression. Unlike earlier, he's changed into a different pair of jeans and a nicer shirt, paired with the same white Air Force 1's I own.

"Alexa? What's wrong?"

He ushers me in, but luckily, there's no other girl inside this time.

"I don't know why I came here," I say faintly. "I'm sorry about earlier, Beau. I was a bitch."

"So, you need a drinking buddy?" He rubs his chin and then grabs his phone off the desk. "I know just the place."

"You know neither one of us are legal?"

"It's not about what you know. It's who you know."

Beau has a friend who happens to be throwing some wicked rooftop party tonight. It is only a few blocks over, making it easy to walk. I know I'm in the right place when I see the keg. I'm not a fan of beer, but there is tequila, and that will work just as well.

"We're doing shots," I tell Beau.

"Really? Because one of us should probably be responsible," he teases, even though he's pouring already. "I guess you deserve a college experience."

I burst out laughing as Beau motions for me to lick my wrist so he can pour salt. The lemon wedges are sitting in front of us in a bowl, next to bowls of chips and pretzels.

"Okay. Three, two, one..." I lick my wrist, throw back the shot and suck on the lemon.

Fuck.

"Damn," Beau lets out a rasp. "The first one hurts the most."

My face is all scrunched up until I open my mouth wide to stop my insides from burning. When it begins to settle, I start to feel more relaxed.

"College life, huh? Daddy would be so proud if I did this instead of studying."

Beau chuckles. "My dad still does this instead of working. He called me drunk yesterday from some work function. I swear I heard stripper music in the background."

"Oh, your mom would have loved that." I chuckle, knowing all too well Rocky and Nikki are so nasty when they fight. "I can imagine the fight now..."

Beau shakes his head with confusion. "I still have no idea how my parents are still married."

I place my hand on his chest. "They've always loved each other. And you know what? They're so perfect for each other, the right balance of obnoxious versus... I don't know how to describe your mom."

"Psychotic?"

"Stop." I laugh, pouring us another drink. "Nikki is a badass."

We do another round, then three more. There's music

playing, so we get up and dance with some group. I have no idea who any of these people are, but damn I feel free. As I sway my arms in the air, breathing it all in, Beau grabs my waist.

"Are you okay?"

I squeeze his cheek to annoy him. "Better than okay."

"That's the tequila talking."

"And? I like the tequila talking."

"Okay, they're gonna shut down this party soon, so I should probably get you back to your hotel."

The moment he says it, my stomach begins to turn. I can't face Hunter, not after our fight. This is exactly why Eric said never to mix business with pleasure. I mixed it, and now it's a whole damn mess.

All because of stupid feelings.

Beau grabs my arm, but his simple touch hurts. I glance down to get a look at why. It's where I knocked myself on the door. My stupid implant moved and is now barely beneath the surface of my skin. I begin to pick at it to remove it since a new one needs to be inserted properly.

"What are you doing?"

"Got a knife?"

"A knife?" Beau rummages in his jeans, producing a small pocketknife.

"Oh my god, why do you have a knife?"

"New York City, baby," he simply says, then rolls his eyes. "I only take it with me at night."

Inside my hand, I quickly flick the knife part open and slice the small piece of skin on my arm.

"Jesus fucking Christ, Alexa!" Beau grabs it off me. "Are you crazy?"

"Can you take it out?" I beg of him, scowling in pain. "Let's count to three."

I start to count, shutting my eyes until Beau rips it out, and I yell out loud, stomping my foot on the ground to shake it off.

"I think you need medical attention." He cringes while moving in to examine it. "There's a lot of blood."

Removing some tissues from my purse, I place them on my arm to stop the bleeding. It doesn't take long for the tissues to soak, so this time I grab a whole stack of napkins from the table to apply pressure. The majority of the pain begins to subside but is still a dull throb.

"I'm fine. The tequila made me numb."

"Look, I'm taking you back to the hotel, okay?"

"Aye, Aye, captain." I nod, then salute him.

Beau laughs. "Fuck, you're wasted."

We take a cab ride back to the hotel, but I spend most of it laughing at Beau and reminiscing about the time his underwear got caught in our cubby house, and my cousin Andy had to cut them to get him out.

"They were my favorite ones too," Beau complains with a pout. "*Toy Story* with Rex all over them."

"I can't believe you remember what was on them!"

The driver pulls up to the hotel, so we pay and get out. As Beau follows me inside, I fumble in my purse for the room key. The hotel staff in the lobby greet us, to which we both wave and try to act sober.

When we reach the floor, I glance at the room numbers, but they appear blurry.

"I think this is me."

"Are you sure? Didn't you say eight-thirty-one?"

"Yeah?"

"This is eight-fourteen," he drags.

"Oh, my bad."

We walk in the opposite direction until we're standing in front of the right room.

"Thanks for tonight. I had fun."

"Thank the tequila." Beau chuckles, tucking his hands into his jeans pocket. "I had fun too."

The door suddenly opens, and Hunter stands in the doorway with a jealous stare. He's still wearing the same suit as earlier, but his eyes are bloodshot, and his hair is a mess. The sleeves of his shirt are rolled up to his elbow. *Why does he have to look so hot?*

"You're here," I say, grinning.

Hunter doesn't say a single word, clenching his jaw with a pinched expression.

"This is Beau Romano. He is Will's brother. So, you're like my brother-in-law? I dunno, let's just say brother." I watch as neither of them says or does anything. "Beau, this is my boss, Hunter Cash."

The tumbleweed tumbles past in an awkward state of silence. Just when I think it's gone, a whole row of them follow. Yeah, this is painful.

"Okay, so this meeting was lovely. I'm going to bed." It suddenly comes to my attention that Beau is seeing me enter Hunter's room. Fuck. I turn to face Beau. "Ah, it's not what you think."

Beau juts his chin with a sneer, then bows his head, unable to look me in the eye. "Doesn't matter what I think, Alexa. It's your life. Have a nice night."

As Beau walks away, a heaviness settles inside my chest. He's right. It didn't matter what anyone thought. It is my life. As long as I'm happy, that's all that matters.

I enter the room and throw my purse onto the table as Hunter closes the door. When I turn around, I raise my hand.

"Whatever you have to say to me can wait until tomorrow," I tell him, suddenly tired from all the drama. "I get it. You're pissed, jealous, whatever. I'm tired, and my stupid arm is now hurting. I want to sleep."

Hunter continues his stance, remaining silent. I fall onto the bed, hugging the pillow. Sleep—it's such a nice feeling. I welcome it with open arms, drifting into a blissful dreamland where everything is just fine.

The next morning, I'm in *hell*.

Every inch of me hurts—my head, my eyes, even my skin. As I sit up, I notice the empty bed, but the sudden movement makes me queasy.

"*Shit.*"

I cover my mouth, running to the bathroom just in time to throw up. My head throbs even more. The only relief is when I rest my head on the tiled wall. I continue to sit this way for maybe thirty minutes, then stumble back to bed.

There's a message on my phone, so I open it quickly.

HUNTER

The car will pick you up at 6 p.m. sharp. Be dressed. I'll meet you there.

I choose not to respond since there's nothing much to say. I'll be right for tonight if I spend the rest of the day hydrating.

Then, if we're up for it, we can talk about what we're doing.

All I know is this can't continue.

Not when I think I'm falling in love with him.

TWENTY-SIX

The black dress I'm wearing is a last-minute favor from Ava and Eric.

Thanks to their connections, the designer dropped it off at my hotel room with matching accessories. The measurements were exact, even surprising me. If Ava and Eric are good for anything, it's their ability to organize an outfit in a heartbeat's notice. I'm pretty sure they have measurements for everyone in our family.

As I enter the large event room, I pull the train of my dress with me since a man accidentally stepped on it in the lobby. The black dress is half-shoulder with a tight-laced bodice and a silk skirt with a slit up my thigh. I wear my hair out as usual but applied more makeup to my eyes. My lipstick is a shade of red, something I haven't done before, but Ava sent me tutorials and then requested I send pics when done. I also needed to cover the cut on my lip.

Since I got the Ava and Eric seal of approval, I consider myself looking very nice tonight.

Standing here by myself is a whole other story. I text

Hunter to see where he is, but he is caught up and running late.

Just fucking great.

I walk around, smiling at people, but then a man stops in front of me.

"You must be Alexandra Edwards?"

His smile is cheesy, and his bald head leaves nothing to the imagination. The tuxedo he is wearing is too big.

I force a polite smile. "Yes, I am. And you are?"

"Chester Jones," he introduces, shaking my hand. His hand is sweaty, but I pretend I don't notice. "I'm head of the East Coast division. We've communicated via email."

"Of course." The name becomes familiar. "It's nice to finally meet you."

"And you. So, Hunter tells me your father is Lex Edwards?"

I tilt my head, swallowing the lump inside my throat. Why would Hunter mention this? He knows I prefer to keep my family life private.

"Yes, he is."

"I understand your father is here tonight to do a speech."

"Oh, really?" I glance around, suddenly panicked.

Chester furrows his brows. "You had no idea?"

"I don't discuss work with my father," I inform him.

"Interesting." Chester moves in closer, making me uncomfortable, especially when his eyes fall to my chest. "Because anything you have access to remains confidential. Big lawsuits would be involved if you leaked to your father exactly what our company is doing."

A chill runs down my spine, followed by a roiling stomach. I carefully choose my words, even though I want to tell this bald motherfucker to go to hell.

"I assure you, I take my work very seriously."

"Good, because don't cry when your father finally gets a taste of his own medicine."

What did he just say?

His lingering bad breath is enough to make me want to hurl. Just when I'm about to excuse myself to the restroom, an alluring scent washes over me. I breathe it all in, then notice Hunter standing beside me.

The tuxedo he is wearing is styled to perfection, making him appear all the sexier. He's freshly shaven, but his eyes appear bloodshot on closer inspection. I observe him with parted lips, but I quickly turn away so Chester doesn't notice.

"It was nice meeting you, Alexandra." Chester musters a phony smile, but soon his expression turns stern. "Cash, we need to talk."

"Later," Hunter informs him.

Thankfully, Chester and his bad breath leave.

"You look beautiful, Alexandra," Hunter mentions but keeps his distance.

"And you look handsome, Mr. Cash."

Our stupid fight yesterday seems even more stupid now. I ache to touch him, but of course, none of that is allowed. People fill the room, making it hard to talk to Hunter privately. For most of the night, he introduces me to people he knows, but of everyone I meet, it's my father I dread running into the most.

"Can we go somewhere for a minute?" I ask, scanning to make sure no one I know sees me.

"Sure."

We quickly weave in and out of the crowd, but just before we exit the main room, my parents are standing in the lobby. My father is dressed in a tuxedo, just like

Hunter's. Mom is wearing a white halter-neck silk gown. Her hair is styled to the side and waved elegantly to show her diamond necklace. As always, she's stunning.

"Fuck," I mumble, taking a deep breath. "My parents are over there."

My father spots me first, leaning down to whisper to Mom, who glances my way. They both walk toward us, making it impossible to ignore them.

"Alexa, honey." Mom reaches out to embrace me. I welcome the hug, missing her so much. "You look beautiful."

"Same for you, Mom."

"Alexa," Dad simply nods before shifting his gaze to Hunter. I know this expression well. He's showing no emotion, but inside, he's already plotting Hunter's death.

"Hi, Dad," is all I say, but then I draw in breath. "I'd like to formally introduce you to my boss, Mr. Cash."

Dad extends his hand, which Hunter shakes with a pressed smile. "I believe we have met."

"We have," Hunter reassures him.

An awkward silence falls between them, so I quickly introduce Mom.

"And, of course, my mother, Charlotte Edwards."

They shake hands politely. "It's nice to meet you, Mrs. Edwards."

Mom smiles graciously, but when she gazes at me oddly, I feel like she can read my mind. There is no chance I'm hanging out with them tonight, so I try to think of some excuse.

"You're here for how many days?" Mom asks.

"Leaving tomorrow."

"I heard you went to NYU to see Beau." Mom grins, but I can tell she knows the whole story. How on Earth, though? "Rocky has a big mouth, in case you're wondering."

I nod, then smile. "Of course. His son sure knows how to surprise me."

"Charlotte, we must say hello to the Prestons. Shall we?"

Mom quickly touches my arm with a warm smile. "If we don't see you again tonight, see you back home, okay?"

"Bye, Mom."

My father simply walks away, taking Mom with him. The second they're gone, I turn to face Hunter.

"You could have been nicer to my dad."

Hunter cocks his head. "Excuse me? Why should I tolerate his behavior? Or should I just continue to smile while your mother talks about how much fun your family is?"

"Hey," I almost shout. "Don't bring my mother into this. Just admit you don't like my father."

"Well, you don't like your father," he argues back.

"You know what? I have no idea what your problem is anymore. You're so hot and cold. I get it, I'm young, and apparently, you're in a fake marriage."

"Alexandra—"

"I need some space," I mumble, desperate to ask him about what Chester said, but I keep quiet. Now is not the time. I'm angry and frustrated, knowing I don't do well in either one of these moods.

There's nowhere to go unless I leave the venue. I glance toward the ceiling, noticing a mezzanine section like those opera booths people sit in. Yanking my dress and lifting it, I make my way to the back stairs and walk up in the dimly lit narrow staircase. When I reach the final step, I move toward the edge.

The view from here is spectacular, with all the lights and people looking stunning in their gowns. The floral arrangements are centered perfectly, but with the dim lights, it looks like some enchanted forest.

I stand here for a while, just observing while thinking about life. Last night with Beau was so much fun. With him, things are easy. We've grown up together, and with that comes a comfort I've been missing.

My mind wanders back to our conversation about college. As I glance around, I realize this doesn't make me happy. All these older people have lived or have their careers. I just want to have fun, not feel the weight of the world on my shoulders, and most of all, I just want to be me again.

An MC comes onto the stage to speak about the origin of this gala. After a rather large applause, he then introduces my father.

As always, Dad stands tall and poised, taking the microphone and knowing he was born to lead. He begins his speech with a story. Surprisingly, I listen with interest.

Then, a hand wraps around my waist, forcing my eyes to close from the smallest of touches. My stomach flutters in anticipation, but at the same time, my heart slowly begins to bleed. What we're doing has no happy ending.

It'll only destroy more people.

"Hunter," I whisper. "Not now."

I can almost smell the whisky on his skin. This is very unlike him. Usually, he is in control, but something has gotten to him. Maybe, it was our fight.

"Alexandra, I need you…"

His hand slides up my thigh, but just as I'm about to push him away, he yanks my panties down.

"We can't here," I warn him. "My father is—"

"You're mine, you understand." His words sound more like a plea. This desperation we both feel even though we know what we're doing is wrong.

You're mine...

The words repeat and explode like dynamite this time, breaking the walls inside me until they crumble into a heap on the ground. I open my mouth to say something, but he manages to enter me, causing me to gasp.

This is wrong. We shouldn't be doing this here.

My body is betraying me, desperately wanting him, but all I can think about is my father talking right over the loud-speaker.

The voices inside me don't stop, all battling with each other to speak the loudest. I desperately craved Hunter's touch, but something has changed between us.

"Family is why I'm here," I hear my father say.

Family... family... the word stabs me in the heart.

A small cry escapes me. I can't do this. At the same time, Hunter pushes forward and groans. He stills his move-ments as I try to fight back my tears. Slowly, he slides himself out and zips up his pants.

As quick as it started, it ended just as fast.

I turn around to face him, fueled by emotions. "Are you trying to destroy my father?"

"Alexandra, what kind of a question is that?"

"Answer me," I demand, glaring at him. "At the board meeting, I saw you hush Carol when she spoke about Harperlex. Earlier tonight, Chester threatened me. He said if I leaked anything to my father about what you're doing as so-called payback, then I'd be fighting a big lawsuit."

Hunter angrily fixes his tux jacket then wipes his mouth

with the back of his hand. He bares his teeth, glaring with cold eyes.

"Jesus fucking Christ, Alexandra. Stop acting like a child. Business is business."

His outburst leaves me speechless. So, he was trying to destroy him all along, so he needed me as bait. I'm nothing more to him than a joke.

"So, then I was bait?" A sharp pain spreads across my chest. "You used me to do what exactly?"

"Don't even go there," he mutters.

"Why? It makes perfect sense that..." I trail off as my brain switches to last night and the removal of my birth control.

You just let him fuck you bareback.

With no protection.

I clutch my stomach, unable to breathe. Nausea has a chokehold on me, making me faint and slightly dizzy. Hunter watches me, but he has no sympathy because, of course, he is just a man.

And I'm the woman who stupidly fell in love with him.

"Whatever we have," I quiver, fighting back the urge to cry. "Is over."

His gaze flickers, nostrils flaring while he runs his hand through his hair. "Don't say that, Alexandra. You just don't understand..."

"Consider this my resignation and termination of whatever you want to call us fucking around with each other behind your wife's back."

"I told you the truth!"

"Yeah," I murmur, fixing my panties since he didn't even bother to pull them back up. "But actions speak louder than words. You want to destroy my father, and I'm the fool who fell for all your tricks. Goodbye, Hunter."

I turn my back with a heavy chest, and the moment I take the first step down the stairs, I cover my mouth and burst out crying.

What the hell have I done to my life?

TWENTY-SEVEN

"I'm not okay."

As Beau sighs on the other end, my soft cry carries over the phone. I didn't know who to call, my sisters felt too far away, and Mom was still at the event. I've never felt more alone in such a big city with millions of people.

"Where are you, Alexa?"

I glance around my room as nostalgia consumes me. I'm lying in the same single bed from when I was a kid. My sisters all had their king-size beds, but I always felt alone in such a large bed, so I would end up sleeping between my parents. When I was about eight, Mom suggested a smaller bed which got me out of their room. As an adult, I now understand why.

The bookshelves still house all my favorite reads plus ornaments I've collected over the years. In each of our homes, a piece of my life sits on the shelves. I remember it all so fondly, when life wasn't complicated, and the world genuinely felt like it was my oyster.

My arms wrap around the teddy bear my father won for

me in Coney Island when I was five years old. It's not the prettiest of bears, given it looks like a Care Bear knockoff. Yet, it still smells of strawberries even after all these years.

"I'm home," I murmur.

"In LA?"

"No, here."

"Okay," Beau says softly. "Just sit tight."

The last few days were exhausting. My life is spinning out of control, and I'm caught in the thick of it. Tears stream down my cheeks as I hold onto this bear as if my life depends on it. My phone pings, but I don't want to talk or even read messages, especially if it's Hunter. Reaching over, I turn the phone off, almost relieved no one else can find me.

My eyes begin to feel heavy from the constant crying. The sirens in the street are like white noise, helping my conscience to fall asleep.

But my dreams soon turn into my nightmare. I'm lying on the bed, fluorescent lights bolted to the ceiling, almost blinding me. I hear things, laughter, and machines, and then the nurse explains exactly what will happen next.

I will fall asleep, and my baby will be gone.

A dry rasp escapes my throat as I sit up, unable to breathe. Beside me, a hand touches my arm softly, forcing me to open my eyes properly.

"Alexa," the voice whispers. "It's going to be okay."

My eyes sting with tears, and the hollowness inside my chest slowly begins to disappear. I reach out to touch my father's hand, and just like the strawberry-scented bear, I don't want to let go.

"I'm sorry, Dad," I cry softly.

There's a soft glow inside the room from my lamp. As my gaze shifts to meet his, I can see his glassy eyes staring back at me. I know he's trying to be strong, but he's struggling.

"There's nothing to be sorry about," he gently tells me. "If anyone should be sorry, it's me. I should have listened to you, but I was scared of losing you."

"I promise you'll never lose me, Dad." I touch his hand and place it on my cheek, just like I would always do as a child. "There was just so much going on. I was scared."

My father gently caresses my cheek. "Alexa, deep breaths. We don't need to discuss it now. There will be the right time when you're ready."

"I screwed up," I whisper. "I hurt you."

A small smile graces Dad's lips, but it's a proud smile. "I'm built strong. Not perfect, but strong. We all screw up. It's called life. There are so many things I did wrong, but the only thing you can do is learn to move on. Life stops for no one. Things happen, and people change. We love, we hurt, but if we're lucky enough, we have each other to get through those hard times."

My chest hitches as I sob uncontrollably, prompting Dad to wrap his arms around me. Inside his embrace, I feel safe. No one can hurt me, not even myself. As I pull back, I notice my mascara run on his shirt.

"Your shirt..."

"I'm used to it," he says, keeping his voice low. "Each of your sisters has cried on me at one point or another. Your mother is probably the worst offender."

I manage a small smile. "The ultimate girl dad."

He stares into my eyes profoundly. "I wouldn't change it for the world."

My arms wrap around him again. It feels like we have years to catch up, and I hate myself for stealing this time away from us. Suddenly, my stomach grumbles. I haven't eaten since lunchtime, given the food at the event rarely came my way before my encounter upstairs with Hunter.

A heavy sigh escapes me, wondering what he is doing right now.

"How about I head out and grab a pizza," he suggests. "Your mother is probably starving too."

"Mom is here?"

"Inside the living room, or maybe outside this door, waiting for the green light to come in and fuss all over you."

My lips curve upward into a smile. "You can send her in."

There are some things I want Dad to know, but some things remain best between us girls.

"Dad," I call softly, fidgeting with the edge of my blanket. "I handed in my resignation tonight. But there is one thing I want to talk to you about. I just don't know how to say it."

He places his hand on mine. "You can tell me anything. Just remember, my silence means I'm processing."

"Do you know Chester Jones?"

A smirk settles on his lips. "Alexa, you don't need to say another word. I know him. I know everything. He's not the first person to try and bring me down, and he won't be the last."

"Okay, I just didn't feel right about the whole thing."

"I may not know anything about being a teenage girl or becoming a woman. I don't understand women's fascination with suits or even gray sweatpants. What I know is business. I wouldn't be where I am today if I wasn't always one step ahead of everyone else."

I quickly grab Dad's arm. "Don't ruin Hunter's company, please?"

It's obvious to see Dad is doing his best to control his

opinions on the subject, given I'd called Hunter by his name and not formally as Mr. Cash. My father is smart enough to figure it out.

"Sweetheart, don't worry about my business." He stands tall to leave the room but stops at the door. "I want you to start living your life the way you want."

Moments later, Mom enters. Unlike Dad, who is fairly controlled, she rushes by my side. Her hug is like a warm blanket on a cold winter's day, filling me with comfort and protection, a safe place to express my thoughts.

"I fell in love with him, Mom. It was different to Cole, you know? It was just so... I don't have the words to explain it."

Mom draws in a breath, then releases slowly. "Consuming."

"Yes, it did consume me. I know I shouldn't compare, but my relationship with Cole felt shallow. It's why..." I trail off, trying to find the strength to tell her the truth. It has to be now. I need help to get through this because doing it alone has been the hardest part of this so-called journey. "Mom, I fell pregnant in senior year."

"Alexa," Mom chokes. "Why didn't you tell me?"

"I was scared, terrified actually. I didn't even tell Cole. He was so excited to go to college, and all I could think about was how this baby with ruin everyone's lives. Cole's, our family, and I was scared to raise a baby on my own and so young."

Mom tightens her grip on my hand. "You would never have been alone. Sure, your father would have been angry at first, but a child is a blessing."

"I... I..." My mouth can't even say the words out loud. "I chose not to keep it."

Without a thought or moment of judgment, Mom hugs me fiercely.

"I knew something happened. I just didn't know what." Mom distances herself but holds my arms in her grip. "I want you to speak to someone, a professional. I know you don't want to do that, but losing a baby, no matter what the circumstances are, can result in long-term trauma."

I nod quietly. "I know, Mom. I was hoping to escape the nightmares, but they always find their way back. When we get back home, I'll see anyone you recommend."

We continue to chat openly, and Mom gives me space to talk about everything I've held back. Soon after, Dad returns with pizza.

As I sit with the two of them, we eat pizza and drink soda while learning how to reconnect without the tension I've grown accustomed to with my father.

"I don't want to start an argument," Dad begins as Mom purses her lips. "You know our home will always be home. Anytime you want, the keys are yours again."

I breathe a sigh of relief, offering a smile. It's exactly what I need to hear, but a part of me wanted to do something else.

At least, I need some time to think.

"Mom, Dad? Do you think we can stay here for another week? There's something I want to do with the both of you."

"Of course, honey. We can rearrange our schedules."

"Good."

Dad tilts his head with a smile. "Are you going to share what it is you'd like us to do together?"

I grin, shaking my head. "Patience, dear father of mine. I need to make sure it's what I want first."

Tonight was too much. I excused myself to bed and told them I needed a few days just to process things. They both offered their support, but I needed to take care of things first.

That included my *heart.*

I didn't lie around, cry, or eat tubs of ice cream, but the pain and heartache never left me. Wherever I went, whatever I saw, memories found their way back, and the heaviness inside my chest became this constant fixture.

When I found the courage to turn my phone on, I was surprised to see nothing at all from Hunter. Not one missed call, not one single text. As for the rest of the messages, I ignored them for now because I needed to do one thing.

Apologize to April.

As I'm about to call her, I hold back. Why would I tell her over the phone if she didn't know? Some things needed to be done in person, and I made a note for it to be the very first thing I do when I'm back in LA.

I knock on the door, tapping my feet impatiently. The door opens, and Beau is standing across from me with a knowing grin.

"You ready?"

With a smile, I nod. I found out Beau was the one who called my father that night. He knew exactly what I needed, and he was right.

I spend the day with Beau, gathering everything I need before meeting with my parents this afternoon. We decide on this cute little café in Chelsea, which is not overly busy if you go there after lunch. Both my parents are working from their Manhattan offices but were able to stay longer at my request.

They both sit across from me as I slide over a folder.

"What's this?" Mom asks.

I draw in a breath, then release with a smile. "I've decided to go to college. Inside this folder is a list of the campuses I've narrowed it down to. I've done my pro and con lists for each one. I know there's no guarantee I'll be accepted, but I would love it if both of you would tour them with me. There are dates listed inside, so I hope they will fit in with your schedule."

My parents continue to sit in silence, neither one of them opening the folder.

"Aren't you going to open the folder?"

Dad slides it back to me. "If this is your decision, we support you wherever you want to go."

I'm taken aback, half expecting him to give me statistics on the four I've narrowed it down to. That's even if I get in, still another hurdle to jump over.

"But the dates?"

"We'll be there no matter what."

That day changed everything. I found myself excited to visit each campus, and eager to learn about the history and culture. I still have no idea what I want to major in, but like a good friend once told me, it'll all just fall into place.

When I get my first official email to attend an interview with the Dean of Admissions, I jump in joy, excited about this new adventure.

With my phone in hand, I go to call my parents but notice a red notification on my calendar. The last few days have been chaotic, meaning I haven't had a chance to catch up on anything on my phone or even respond to anyone.

I click on the app, but then my mouth falls open as my limbs turn numb.

Period overdue...

To be continued...

CRAVING US

**The Secret Love Series
Book 2**

Beau Romano

I am *not* in love with Alexa Edwards.

I don't fall in love with girls. No, not me. I fuck them when I need, then find someone else when I'm bored.

But ever since she moved to Manhattan, things have changed. We've started hanging out more, doing things I normally don't do with girls.

If possible, she's become more beautiful. How, I have no idea. I just can't stop thinking about her.

It's driving me insane.

There's only one person who knows and possibly the most annoying person in the world.

"Son, I warned you about too much pussy." Dad huffs, then places his hand on my shoulder. "Too much, and you get bored. Once you're bored, you start searching for something else."

"C'mon, Dad," I drag. "There's no such thing as too much pussy."

"Trust me, there is."

This is all very rich coming from the man who constantly taunts my mother that he is the hottest thing alive and can get any woman he wants. I've seen him in action, and so has Mom. Anytime any other woman goes near him, he freaks and shows his wedding ring. Quite frankly, it's fucking hilarious that even Mom makes fun of it.

But my problem is not over too much pussy as Dad likes to put it. My problem is I'm kind of, sort of, falling for a woman who has no interest in me.

To Alexa, I'm just her annoying friend or as she likes to call me, brother from another mother. She's totally friend-zoned me.

And I know exactly why.

She's still in love with *him*.

Even though the media has published articles saying he's expecting a baby with his wife.

ALSO BY KAT T. MASEN

The Dark Love Series

Featuring Lex & Charlie

Chasing Love: A Billionaire Love Triangle

Chasing Us: A Second Chance Love Triangle

Chasing Her: A Stalker Romance

Chasing Him: A Forbidden Second Chance Romance

Chasing Fate: An Enemies-to-Lovers Romance

Chasing Heartbreak: A Friends-to-Lovers Romance

Lex: A Companion Novella

Charlotte: A Companion Novella

The Forbidden Love Series

(The Dark Love Series Second Generation)

Featuring Amelia Edwards

The Trouble With Love: An Age Gap Romance

The Trouble With Us: A Second Chance Love Triangle

The Trouble With Him: A Secret Pregnancy Romance

The Trouble With Her: A Friends-to-Lovers Romance

The Trouble With Fate: An Enemies-to-Lovers Romance

The Secret Love Series

(The Dark Love Series Second Generation)

Featuring Alexandra Edwards

Craving Love: An Age Gap Romance

Craving Us: A Second Chance Romance

Craving Her: A Friends-to-Lovers Romance

Also by Kat T. Masen

The Pucking Arrangement: A Stepbrother Romance

The Office Rival: An Enemies-to-Lovers Romance

The Marriage Rival: An Office Romance

Bad Boy Player: A Brother's Best Friend Romance

Roomie Wars Box Set (Books 1 to 3): Friends-to-Lovers Series

ABOUT THE AUTHOR

Kat T. Masen is a USA Today Bestselling Author from Sydney, Australia. Her passion is writing angsty love triangles involving forbidden men like besties older brother.

She is also the founder of the Books Ever After store, Books By The Bridge Author Events, and spends way too much time on Tik Tok creating videos for her #1 Amazon bestseller Chasing Love.

Oh... and she's a total boy mom.
1 husband, 4 boys, and a needy pug.

Download free bonus content, purchase signed paperbacks & bookish merchandise.
Visit: **www.kattmasen.com**

Made in United States
Troutdale, OR
11/07/2023

14363513R00163